STANDARDS FOR THE DEVELOPMENT OF ARCHIVES SERVICES IN IRELAND

STANDARDS FOR THE DEVELOPMENT OF ARCHIVES SERVICES IN IRELAND

Published in 1997 by
The Society of Archivists Irish Region,
Bishop Street, Dublin 8, Ireland.

British Library Cataloging in Publication Data available.

ISBN 0 - 7165 - 2620 - 4

Text:	The Society of Archivists Irish Region
Index:	Julitta Clancy
Photography:	Lorcaqn Farrell Hugh Glynn
Design:	Ger Garland
Printing:	Colour Books
Distribution:	Irish Academic Press
Orders:	Irish Academic Press at Gill & Macmillan Distribution Goldenbridge, Inchicorr, Dublin 8.

The Archives Service

The Archivist: Professional Code & Strategies

The Archives: Control & Processing

The Repository

FOREWORD

In October 1993 the Irish Region of the Society of Archivists held a one day seminar on Archival Standards. The speakers came from Britain and Ireland, recognised experts in their fields, and the attendance was drawn from all over Ireland. The response of the audience was most positive and much fruitful discussion and exchange of ideas took place.

The seminar had been held to highlight the work of a sub-committee within the Irish Region which had been established the previous year. The want of an Irish archival standard had long been felt and the committee of the Irish Region had responded positively to the request of some of its members to initiate work in identifying and detailing professional standards relating to all aspects of archival work within the Irish context. The one-day seminar was the first formal recognition of the work of the sub-committee.

Based on the response to the seminar the work on an Irish archival standard continued apace. Members of the Irish Region gave most freely of their time and expertise to draw up such an Irish standard. The results are now laid before the public.

Up until the present there was no Irish standard relating to archives in Ireland. Developments were based on British and international standards and practices. Now for the first time Ireland has a standard of its own. This is now brought before the public to assist and guide it in all aspects of developments dealing with the creation, preservation and management of archives and an archives service in Ireland.

The Chairman and Committee of the Irish Region of the Society of Archivists cannot express sufficiently their gratitude to those members who have worked so diligently on the present publication. The thanks of the whole of the Irish Region must be extended to Mary Clark, Ailsa C. Holland, Frances McGee, Thomas Quinlan, David Sheehy and Virginia Teehan for their commitment to the production of an Irish archival standard and for their efforts in bringing the work and deliberations of the sub-committee to publication standard.

Further thanks must be extended to Ger Garland for design and layout, to Julitta Clancy for indexing and to the Irish Academic Press with which the Irish Region has for so long been associated. The support of the Society of Archivists must also be acknowledged.

It is to be hoped that *Standards for the Development of Archives Services in Ireland* will reach as wide an audience as possible and that those already engaged in the creation and preservation of archives, or those about to contemplate such a move, will find in this publication a vital reference work and one of inestimable assistance to them.

Aideen M. Ireland
Chairman

Introduction

Archives are a great national resource. They document the historical evolution and identity of the communities living on this island, they protect the interests of institutions and society, and they constitute a valuable source of information to be used and enjoyed for generations to come.

The publication of a second edition of *Directory of Irish Archives* in 1993 was testimony to the continuing expansion of archives services in Ireland. Expansion has been boosted by the passage of the National Archives Act in 1986, by the Local Government Act in 1994 and by a growing awareness in Irish society of the need to preserve and to utilise its archival heritage.

Standards for the development of archives services in Ireland has been produced by the Irish Region of the Society of Archivists, which is the professional association for archivists in Ireland. It is a response to the growth of archives services in recent years in both the public and private sectors. Indications are that the number of archives services will increase in the future and that existing services are likely to expand. It is important that standards are articulated which will help shape the establishment and expansion of these services.

The standards have two objectives. Firstly, they will guide institutions and organisations wishing to establish archives services and will help to ensure that they are properly constituted and staffed, and that the range and nature of the services provided by the archivist are fully understood. Secondly, the standards are designed to support the work of the archivist by outlining what the archivist does and detailing the infrastructure required to achieve the archivist's principal commitments of managing records, preserving archives and making them available to society. It must be emphasised that these standards are not intended as an operational manual.

Information technology is having a dramatic impact on the records archivists manage today and the archives they will preserve tomorrow. It also influences the daily management of archives services, the ways in which archivists communicate and the options they have in disseminating information about what they preserve. As ideas are constantly evolving in these areas and as professional opinions about procedures are effervescent, archivists must continue to participate in discussions and experiment with information technology until broadly conclusive standards are reached by the profession. It did not seem wise at this point in time to deal with information technology at length in the context of this publication.

Records management services are versatile and are shaped by the structure and function of individual institutions and whether these are in the public, private or commercial sectors. It seemed appropriate at this stage in the development of Irish archives to deal with the subject in broad outline and to restrict detail to essentials in order to maintain a balance within the standards. Another area which will demand greater attention at a future date is that of specialised media such as film, photographic and sound archives.

These standards, the first of their kind in Ireland, were compiled by archivists representing a broad range of archives services: national, local authority, university and specialist. An emphasis has been placed on practical issues, on those aspects of the work of the archivist and the archives service which are most germane to the development of archives services in Ireland at the present, and on keeping the publication within a reasonable size. It will undoubtedly be necessary to issue a second edition of these standards early in the new millennium to take account of developments within Irish archives services, within the profession and within archival science.

The members of the Standards Sub-committee of the Irish Region of the Society of Archivists wish to express their thanks for the assistance they received from the following: The National Archives, Dublin Corporation, University College Cork, University College Dublin, and the Archbishop of Dublin. They also acknowledge with gratitude the support of the officers and members of the Irish Region.

Mary Clark
Ailsa C. Holland
Frances McGee
Tom Quinlan
David Sheehy
Virginia Teehan

The Archives Service

1. *OBJECTIVES*

1.1 Information is one of the oldest and most powerful resources created by the human race. Archives and records contain information. The principal objective of an archives service is to manage both records and archives in order to ensure their most effective and appropriate protection, preservation and organisation.

1.2 An archives service operates with specific strategies which help to realise the full potential of information as a resource whether it is contemporary in nature *(records)* and of use to administration, or whether it has aged *(archives)* and is of use to a wide range of researchers.

1.3 These strategies include:

- the identification of those archives which constitute a unique and valuable source of information;
- the permanent preservation of archives under optimum conditions which ensure that they are physically and morally protected;
- the promotion of the information contained in archives in a variety of ways for the purpose of knowledge, research and legal protection, thus benefitting the organisation in which the archives originated, society and posterity;
- the management of current and non-current records for the purposes of organisational convenience and efficiency;
- the disposition of non-current records either by destruction or by preservation by an archives service;

1.4 The success of an archives service in achieving its objectives is greatly dependent on its sound constitution *(see section 2)*, on the provision of appropriate human and financial resources *(see sections 3 and 6)*, and on effective management *(see section 5)*.

1.5 To achieve the objectives of an archives service, the archivist, operating under a code of professional practice *(see section 8)*, designs and implements wide-ranging strategies *(see sections 9 - 13)*.

2. *ESTABLISHMENT AND CONSTITUTION*

2.1 The establishment of an archives service requires motivation at a high level within an organisation. It also requires the advice of a professional archivist who can survey its records and archives, report on the feasibility and scope of the project and advise on key issues such as the wording and content of the directive which establishes the service.

2.2 The establishment of an archives service should be the subject of a directive approved at the highest level in the organisation to which the service is attached.

2.3 The directive should define both records and archives in terms of their origin, nature and physical attributes.

2.4 The directive should indicate the purpose, objectives and jurisdiction of the archives service, the authority under which it operates and the functions and responsibilities of the archivist. It should provide the archivist with the necessary legal authority and standing to implement all the objectives of the archives service. The nature of the archivist's functions should be clear, thus avoiding any possible confusion with functions more appropriately carried out by other information scientists.

2.5 The directive should identify the officer within the organisation to whom the archivist reports. This officer should be placed at a high level within the organisation, at the centre of its operations and might also, by tradition or by law, have a fundamental responsibility for records. Officers in other information services, or in ancillary branches of an organisation, do not provide the appropriate infrastructure for a successful archives service.

2.6 The directive should establish the archivist's relationship with other employees in the organisation by seeking their cooperation in achieving the objectives of the service and in following any guidelines or procedures devised by the archivist for this purpose.

2.7 The directive should establish the archivist's indisputable responsibility to identify and preserve archives, to authorise the destruction of records which have no long term value and to act as final arbiter in all matters affecting the physical and moral protection of archives *(see sections 10 - 11)*.

2.8 The directive might establish an advisory committee, representative of various interest groups and expertise, to support the objectives and policies of the archives service and to foster its development.

2.9 Occasionally, a well established archives service may need to re-examine its fundamental objectives and operations for purposes of reconstitution, expansion or improvement.

3. *PROFESSIONAL, TECHNICAL AND ANCILLARY STAFF*

3.1 Archives services can be categorised as small, medium, large and national. A small archives service could be one attached to an organisation such as a small business company, a corporate body or a religious congregation. A medium-sized archives service could be one attached to a bank, a university or to a local authority with a limited geographic jurisdiction, such as a corporation. A large archives service could be one attached to a county council and a national archives service is one attached to central government.

3.2 The archives service must be in the charge of a professionally qualified archivist.

3.3 To function effectively a small archives service requires a minimum staffing structure of one archivist, one archives assistant and one paper-keeper/porter. The staffing structure would need to increase at some grades in a medium-sized archives service and at all grades in a large archives service. Medium and large-sized archives services may also require clerical and secretarial assistants, all of whom work under the direction and supervision of the archivist.

3.4 The archivist is responsible for formulating policies, designing strategies, setting standards, managing the daily operations of the archives service, and for those functions for which the archivist alone is specifically trained, including appraisal of records to identify their long term value, identification of record groups and collections of archives, design of a finding aid system and processing of collections of archives, and the establishment of policies and standards in all matters relating to the archives service.

3.5 The archives assistant works under the direction and supervision of the archivist carrying out ancillary and support functions thus providing the archivist with the flexibility and mobility essential to professional work. The paper-keeper/porter works under the direction and supervision of the archivist.

3.6 An archives service requires conservators, technicians and computer experts on an occasional, regular or permanent basis depending on its size and on the nature of the archives it preserves. Where such personnel are not available on a permanent basis, sufficient funds must be budgeted to permit employment on a contract basis. Their work is carried out under the direction and supervision of the archivist.

3.7 Additional staff will also be required in the administration of a records centre when a records management service is provided by the archives service *(see section 30).*

3.8 When staff are being recruited for the archives service, the archivist should provide comprehensive job descriptions indicating the requisite qualifications and personal qualities and should participate in interview and selection procedures. Those who work at any grade in an archives service must be of a suitable calibre and must possess a keen sense of responsibility.

3.9 It may be necessary on occasion to employ consultants with a particular expertise where that expertise does not exist among the personnel of the archives service, or does not exist to a sufficient extent to meet all the objectives of the service. Advice of consultants may be necessary on matters such as architecture and engineering, conservation, legal questions, information technology, exhibition design, education, marketing and public relations.

3.10 Volunteers and persons on work-experience or training schemes must not be used as an alternative to the employment of professional and support staff in an archives service.

4. *APPOINTMENT, GRADING AND PROFESSIONAL DEVELOPMENT OF THE ARCHIVIST*

4.1 The archivist must be a graduate of a third level educational institution and possess a professional qualification from an archives training course approved by the Society of Archivists or by an equivalent body in other European Union member states. Qualifications in librarianship, or in any other branch of the information sciences, or research experience are not acceptable alternative qualifications under any circumstance. It is strongly recommended that employers request to see the original degree(s) and diploma conferred on any archivist whose employment is under consideration.

4.2 It is strongly recommended that the archivist is a member of a professional association such as the Society of Archivists or an equivalent body in other

EU member states. A senior position may dictate that the archivist should also possess a number of years experience or be a registered member of the Society of Archivists.

4.3 In recruiting archivists, the following personal qualities must be sought: adherence to a code of professional conduct *(see section 8 and appendix 2)*, discretion, capacity to design and implement professional policy and strategies, communication skills (both written and verbal), ability to work alone and/or as part of a team.

4.4 The principal channels of recruitment for archivists are by advertisements in national newspapers and in the Society of Archivists Career Opportunities circular, by recruitment through the registers of professional archivists maintained by the Irish Region of the Society of Archivists and by the Archives Department, University College Dublin.

4.5 It is not appropriate to recruit archivists through other professional associations or to advertise posts for *archivist/librarian* or *archivist/curator* which will attract unskilled and uninformed applicants.

4.6 The archivist should be appointed at a suitable grade within the organisation to which the archives service is attached. The grade should vary with the level of personal accountability and professional responsibility of the archivist.

4.7 A larger archives service should be structured to allow for promotion within that service. Consideration should be given to the promotion of archivists to higher grades with reference to years of service, expertise acquired, personal qualities and perception of the value of the archivist and the services provided.

4.8 Where an archivist is the sole source of professional expertise within an organisation, there should be a regular salary review.

4.9 The archivist should be encouraged and permitted to attend seminars and training courses, both in Ireland and abroad for the purpose of professional development and registration with the Society of Archivists. The archives service's annual budget should allow for this.

5. *MANAGEMENT AND DEVELOPMENT*

5.1 The archivist is responsible for the day-to-day management of the archives service and is answerable to a designated senior officer within the organisation to which the service is attached.

5.2 The archivist adheres to a code of professional practice in the management of the archives service *(see section 8).*

5.3 The archivist is responsible for outlining the objectives of the service, formulating policy, establishing parameters, setting standards, identifying priorities and communicating information about these both inside and outside the archives service.

5.4 The archivist should be regarded as the final arbiter with reference to questions which arise concerning the identification and acquisition of archives, the use of archives, the physical conditions under which archives are stored, conserved, used, handled and reproduced, the removal of archives from the strongrooms and the management of records.

5.5 The archivist provides a strategic plan for the archives service every five years.

5.6 The archivist provides a report each year on the work of the archives service.

5.7 The archivist provides in-house training and instruction for archives assistants, technicians and paper-keepers and establishes conservation standards for conservators to enable them to contribute fully to the archives service.

5.8 The archivist provides a forum in which the staff members of the archives service can meet on a regular basis to air their views and help contribute to coherent strategies and unified policies.

6. *FINANCE AND BUDGET*

6.1 The establishment of an archives service requires capital expenditure for the provision and equipping of accommodation for the storage and administration of archives.

6.2 Annual budgets, for current expenditure, are required to cover the cost of the archives service, including salaries and wages, equipment and maintenance, information technology development, postal and telecommunication services, conservation and storage, public and researcher services, reception and office expenses, audio-visual expenses and reprographics, conference and professional development, travel expenses and service contracts.

6.3 The archivist is responsible for drawing up annual estimates and overseeing expenditure of the budget.

6.4 It is increasingly the practice for organisations to seek funding and sponsorship from external sources for specific archival strategies and projects. It should be noted that securing such funding and sponsorship is often time-consuming and unrewarding. The practice should only be relied upon for specific strategies or for projects of limited duration. It should not be used as a substitute for the adequate financial subvention of an archives service by the organisation to which it is attached, or as an alternative to the provision of an adequate annual budget.

7. *INFORMATION TECHNOLOGY AND ARCHIVES*

7.1 Information technology is an essential tool in the management of the archives service. In addition to routine administration, it is used by the archivist to carry out specialist functions such as processing archival material and the production of finding aids. However, the preservation of archival integrity and respect for the unique nature of archival material must not be undermined by the technical constraints imposed by computer systems.

7.2 The archivist should be provided with equipment and software which meets the latest standards and which should be regularly reviewed and updated.

7.3 The archivist must have the resources to engage information technology experts to help in the selection of computer systems which meet the requirements of the archives service.

7.4 The archives service should have access to large communicating systems, such as JANET and the Internet.

7.5 Staff of the archives service must be trained to use available information technology facilities as appropriate.

The Archivist: Professional Code & Strategies

8. *PROFESSIONAL CODE*

8.1 The archivist identifies with the objectives of the organisation to which the archives service is attached.

8.2 The archivist utilises human and financial resources to their full potential in order to achieve the objectives of the service.

8.3 The archivist is responsible for the permanent preservation of the archives of the parent organisation and archives from other sources placed in the custody of the archives service; guarding them against loss, theft, alteration and physical damage.

8.4 The archivist preserves the integrity of archives, thus ensuring that their evidential value is not destroyed, altered or fragmented.

8.5 The archivist guards the information contained in archives against unauthorised access, use and disclosure.

8.6 The archivist participates in providing a service for the parent organisation in the management of its records.

8.7 The archivist provides a service for the public by promoting and facilitating the use and display of archives in accordance with the policy of the parent organisation, under acceptable professional standards and in an impartial manner. The archivist seeks to ensure that the policy of the parent organisation on access is an enlightened one.

8.8 The archivist actively promotes the acquisition of archives both within the parent organisation and from other sources, giving due recognition to those who place collections of archives in the custody of the archives service and taking cognisance of their wishes by entering into deposit agreements with them.

8.9 The archivist utilises information technology without lowering professional standards of arrangement and description.

8.10 The archivist promotes the profile of the archives service, both by the exercise of professional standards and by suitable public relations strategies.

8.11 The archivist ensures that the activities of the service do not breach laws relating to archives, export, copyright, data protection or other relevant legislation and regulations within the national jurisdiction and the European Union.

8.12 The archivist does not abuse the position of custodian of archives to promote personal research interests at the expense of other researchers who do not share the archivist's ease of access to archives or privileged understanding of their content.

8.13 The archivist does not abuse a position of trust as custodian of archives for personal financial gain at the expense of the parent organisation or of those who have placed collections of archives in the keeping of the archives service.

8.14 The archivist strives to become informed of changes and developments in archival science, records management and information technology through professional literature and by attendance at conferences, seminars and training courses.

9. *PRESERVATION OF ARCHIVES*

The principal objectives and strategies are

9.1 to provide a secure, environmentally correct and properly equipped storage facility which is used exclusively for the storage of archives;

9.2 to identify and secure those records of the parent organisation which should be preserved permanently by the archives service because of their long term value;

9.3 to identify and acquire collections of archives from other sources for permanent preservation by the archives service in accordance with its acquisition policy and to enter into deposit agreements with the organisations and individuals from whom such collections of archives are acquired;

9.4 to design strategies by which electronic records can be identified for permanent preservation on suitable storage media early in their life cycle;

9.5 to preserve archives permanently in their original form or in any other form identified by the archivist which is compatible with permanent preservation.

10. *MORAL PROTECTION OF ARCHIVES*

The principal objectives and strategies are

10.1 to safeguard the integrity of archives in order to protect the reliability of the evidence they contain;

10.2 to utilise appraisal procedures which facilitate integrity by providing the archivist with a comprehensive understanding of the nature and relationship of those documents or series of documents under review;

10.3 to acquire collections of archives in a manner which ensures that they are not physically fragmented and that parts of collections are not indiscriminately destroyed or wantonly ignored;

10.4 to prevent unauthorised amendment or alteration to any document once it has been acquired by the archives service, or placed in its custody;

10.5 to identify and arrange collections of archives in a manner which is compatible with their provenance;

10.6 to provide researchers with finding aids which permit the critical assessment of the integrity and the evidential reliability of the documents within each collection of archives.

11. *PHYSICAL PROTECTION OF ARCHIVES*

The physical protection of archives requires an integrated preservation policy with the following objectives and strategies:

11.1 to identify and implement strategies to prevent loss or damage of archives in storage, handling, use, reproduction and display and to prevent unauthorised amendment;

11.2 to dictate standards for the storage, handling, use, reproduction, display and conservation of archives;

11.3 to select suitable media or methods of reproduction when substitution copies of documents are necessary as the sole option in preserving permanently the information the original documents contain;

11.4 to prevent alteration of the physical integrity of a document once it has been acquired by the archives service, except under the circumstances outlined in 11.3 or when conservation requirements dictate essential change;

11.5 to assess the conservation needs of archives, to employ professional expertise for the repair, binding and conservation treatment of documents and to set the standard by which this work is carried out;

11.6 to authorise the temporary removal of archives from the jurisdiction of the archives service when necessary and to ensure that correct conditions prevail for their storage, use, display, handling and security;

11.7 to provide and implement a disaster prevention and response plan for the archives service;

11.8 to implement a security microfilming programme for the archives service;

11.9 to provide annually a period of closure in the archives service for the purpose of stocktaking, security and conservation analysis *(see 25.3.3)*.

12. *AVAILABILITY OF ARCHIVES*

The principal objectives and strategies are

12.1 to make archives available for research to members of the public and to members of the organisation of which the archivist is an employee, in accordance with its access policy and that of its various divisions, in accordance with deposit agreements as they apply to collections of archives acquired from other sources, and in accordance with any relevant legislation;

12.2 to exercise discretion by ensuring that documents or data elements which are sensitive in content, which infringe the privacy of the individual, which could cause embarrassment, danger or distress to a living individual, or which concern confidential matters, security or any other point of concern to the organisation of which the archivist is an employee, or to a depositor who has placed archives in the archivist's custody, are not prematurely or inappropriately released for research or public scrutiny;

12.3 to process all collections of archives before they are made available for research;

12.4 to exercise discretion in the admission of researchers in order to ensure that neither documents nor the information they contain are abused;

12.5 to provide access to archives during a period of hours each week which is compatible with the level of support staff and the commitments of the professional staff;

12.6 to provide a research room and other facilities where those engaged in research can consult documents under conditions which permit supervision, the safe handling of documents and the use of recording equipment *(see section 26)*;

12.7 to provide a range of finding aids which promote access to and an understanding of archives *(see 17.3 - 4)*;

12.8 to provide information for researchers on the correct manner in which archives should be handled and to ensure that this standard is adhered to when documents are consulted;

12.9 to ensure that the reproduction of documents is carried out in a manner compatible with their physical integrity and conservation, copyright law and reproduction rights, and to impose restrictions on reproduction when necessary *(see section 27)*;

12.10 to provide general guidance for researchers on the use and diplomatic of documents;

12.11 to promote the use and understanding of archives through various publications, including guides, administrative histories and promotional leaflets *(see section 36 and also appendix 1 for a list of archival publications)*;

12.12 to provide or to participate in the provision of educational facilities, services and related publications *(see section 38)*;

12.13 to organise exhibitions and to facilitate the display of archives under correct conditions *(see section 37)*.

13. RECORDS MANAGEMENT

The principal objectives and strategies are

13.1 to assist in formulating and implementing policy for a records management service for the parent organisation;

13.2 to ensure that the records management service extends to all forms of documentation - paper, electronic, micrographic and other forms;

13.3 to provide advice on the creation and organisation of current records;

13.4 to provide advice on the choice of medium on which information is created and stored;

13.5 to provide advice on the physical form and quality of materials used in the creation of records;

13.6 to provide advice on the design and implementation of a vital records protection programme;

13.7 to participate in the drawing up of schedules which ensure the retention and disposition of non-current records;

13.8 to provide advice on the administration of a records centre for the storage of non-current records;

13.9 to ensure the security of non-current records and facilitate their retrieval by their creating offices when required;

13.10 to ensure that those non-current records which should be preserved permanently are identified and their integrity protected;

13.11 to ensure that electronic records which are to be preserved permanently are identified at the earliest possible time and transferred to a suitable medium;

13.12 to facilitate the continuing use of those records which are preserved permanently and to promote them as a valuable resource within the organisation *(see sections 29 - 31)*.

The Archives: Control & Processing

14. ACQUISITION POLICY

14.1 Archives services acquire archives on the basis of an acquisition policy. The policy may be defined by statute, by tradition, by organisational decision or by geographic factors. It will permit an archives service to acquire archives of specific origin, relating to defined subjects or created within a specific geographical area.

14.2 Archives services should cooperate in the acquisition of collections, in directing intending depositors to appropriate archives services and in ensuring that collections are preserved and not lost through neglect or inactivity. Acquisition policies should be mutually respected.

14.3 Archivists should scrutinise carefully the provenance and ownership or any document or collection of archives offered for sale or donated to the service.

15. APPRAISAL

15.1 Archives are preserved for administrative, legal, research, historical and intrinsic reasons. Appraisal is a procedure which identifies those records or documents which should be preserved permanently as archives. It is a complex procedure and must be carried out only by the archivist.

15.2 Appraisal might occur during field work before a collection of archives is acquired, during the initial treatment of a collection after accessioning, or when a collection is being processed *(see sections 16 - 17)*. In records management practice, the appraisal of non-current records is facilitated by the use of schedules and other appraisal strategies *(see 29.4)*.

16. ACCESSIONING AND RELATED PROCEDURES

16.1 When a collection of archives is acquired by an archives service, it is immediately accessioned, details are entered in an accession register and it is given a reference code.

16.2 To avoid loss or theft of documents, security marking of documents may be carried out at this stage.

16.3 A number of other procedures are then carried out. These ensure that the collection is dry, clean and free from active mould growth and insect infestation before being placed in a strongroom. A preliminary conservation analysis of the collection is made and documents in need of immediate treatment are noted. The documents may then be placed in boxes bearing the collection reference code to await processing. Other procedures must be carried out to ensure that the original order of the documents is maintained and to prevent separate collections becoming intermingled.

Archives in disorder and poor storage conditions, before accession by the archives service

16.4 The precise location of the collection in the strongrooms is recorded in a location index or list, and a shelf list, showing what is contained in each box by order of shelf code, is also compiled.

16.5 The information contained in the accession register, conservation analysis and the location list may be maintained on computer and a database application is particularly useful here.

16.6 Transfer lists, which accompany archives from the organisation of origin, and box lists, which are compiled for incoming collections at the time of accessioning, function primarily as a receipt for accessioning and administrative purposes. They are not an alternative to the descriptive list and to other finding aids. Consequently they should not be used in the research room.

17. *PROCESSING*

17.1 SCOPE

17.1.1 All collections of archives must be fully processed by the archivist before they are made available for research.

17.1.2 Processing concerns the arrangement of a collection of archives, the meticulous description of documents to produce a list and the compilation of a range of other finding aids *(see 17.3 - 4).*

17.1.3 The processing of a collection of archives safeguards its integrity, which in turn guarantees its value and reliability as a body of evidence *(see section 10).*

A recently acquired collection before any work has been carried out

(below) Work in progress on a collection

17.1.4 A descriptive list of the collection which clearly indicates its provenance, system of arrangement and content helps researchers to assess the collection as a primary source, to judge the evidential value of the documents and to locate documents of specific interest to their research topic.

17.1.5 In processing a collection of archives, the archivist has the opportunity to identify documents which are sensitive, confidential or potentially embarrassing in content and to take measures to ensure that they are not prematurely released for research.

17.1.6 The archivist also has the opportunity at this stage to decide on the most suitable packing and storage for the collection, to identify documents which are in need of conservation treatment, to withdraw documents which are too fragile for use and to make arrangements for substitution copies while conservation is in progress.

17.1.7 The archivist also has the opportunity to identify documents which are ephemeral in content, or which have no long term value and to make arrangements for their disposal.

17.1.8 It is becoming increasingly common for standards, particularly descriptive standards, to be used in processing. Standards of this kind, however welcome, are not necessarily suitable for uncritical application to every type of collection and to every type of document.

17.2 ARRANGEMENT

17.2.1 By arranging a collection of archives the relationship between documents is established and their evidential value is protected *(see section 10)*.

17.2.2 The arrangement of each collection of archives will reflect its individuality and unique nature.

Further stage in work in progress on a collection

17.2.3 The arrangement of a collection of archives is based on an intimate understanding by the archivist of its provenance, its original system of arrangement, and of the structure and nature of the surviving archival material. It is not acceptable to impose a system of arrangement on a collection without having first established an understanding of the relationship between those documents which form the collection.

17.2.4 It is not acceptable to arrange collections of similar origin in a predetermined system unless it is considered to be absolutely compatible with their integrity. In view of the individuality and unique nature of most collections of archives, the indiscriminate application of pre-determined systems of arrangement should be avoided. Arrangement by artificial categories is inappropriate and seriously impairs critical and effective use of the collection by researchers.

17.2.5 It is not acceptable under any circumstances to impose systems devised for the classification of library books on archives.

17.3 THE DESCRIPTIVE LIST

17.3.1 A descriptive list is produced for each collection of archives by the archivist as a result of processing.

17.3.2 In the descriptive list each document is described in an accurate manner, the relationship between documents is clearly established, the overall system of arrangement is clarified, and the nature, acquisition and appraisal of the collection is explained.

17.3.3 The descriptive list permits researchers to assess the integrity of the collection, to judge the evidential value of the documents it contains and to understand their implications as primary sources.

17.3.4 The descriptive list permits both researchers and archivists to identify documents of relevance to their specific research interests or professional requirements.

17.3.5 The descriptive list is an important security mechanism because it identifies documents precisely and notes the number of pages they contain. Its compilation also results in the systematic numbering and sub-numbering of all items in the collection.

17.3.6 The descriptive list may form the basis of other finding aids and publications *(see 17.4 and section 36).*

17.4 FINDING AID NETWORK

17.4.1 Archives services must provide a finding aid network to facilitate access to archives by researchers and to provide a means by which archives can be understood.

17.4.2 Finding aids are produced by the archivist in the course of processing collections of archives.

17.4.3 A general index is an essential finding aid which creates access to descriptive lists by proper name, place name and subject matter.

17.4.4 Finding aids which open up access to non-written archives such as maps, photographs, film and sound recordings with reference to their production, technical and artistic features are increasingly essential.

17.4.5 Other finding aids may be desirable such as specialised indexes and sectional lists. Priorities in their compilation are dictated by the nature of the collections preserved by a particular archives service.

17.5 COMPUTER APPLICATIONS & FINDING AID PRODUCTION

17.5.1 It is possible to produce and maintain most finding aids in a computerised format.

17.5.2 Computerisation has obvious advantages in terms of ease of searching, speed of information retrieval and potential for networking locally, nationally and internationally.

17.5.3 It must be noted that the automation of finding aids is still largely experimental, with many packages and different forms of software are being used by archivists worldwide.

17.5.4 It is not acceptable to sacrifice standards in descriptive practice or standards in the arrangement of archives because of the limitations of computer software.

17.5.5 Computers are a valuable tool in the production of finding aids, but are not of themselves a substitute for the skill and expertise of the professional archivist.

17.5.6 The use of non-professional staff utilising computers is only acceptable for listing routine record series and this work must be supervised by an archivist.

The Repository

18. *ROLE AND FUNCTIONS*

18.1 A repository is a building which houses archives and provides accommodation for professional, administrative, technical and public services. The function of the repository is to enable the archives service to achieve its stated objectives *(see section 1)*.

18.2 Once a decision has been taken in principle by the parent organisation that a repository is required, an archivist must be consulted at all stages of the project, from site selection to finished repository.

18.3 Advice must be sought from an architect and structural engineer at an early stage in the planning process. The advice of a structural engineer is particularly important when a building is being adapted for the housing of archives.

19. *TYPES OF BUILDING*

19.1 An archives service may be housed in a purpose-built repository or in a specially adapted existing building.

19.2 A repository which is purpose-built is likely to require higher capital expenditure than a repository in an adapted building. However, maintenance costs for a purpose-built repository are likely to be lower than those for a repository in an adapted building.

19.3 A repository which is purpose-built will usually offer better storage conditions and increased protection against fire than a repository in an adapted building.

19.4 A repository may be obliged to share premises with another service, such as a museum or local history library. In such cases, the repository must be self-contained and protected from other users of the building *(see 22.2 and 23.6)* and the technical requirements laid down for strongrooms must be adhered to.

19.5 Regardless of whether a repository is purpose-built, adapted, or installed as part of shared premises, all relevant legal and regulatory requirements at national and local level in the Republic of Ireland and Northern Ireland must be observed *(see appendix 1)*.

20. SITE SELECTION

20.1 The repository should not be located in an industrial zone because of the attendant dangers of air pollution or in any zone where hazardous activities incompatible with the preservation of archives take place.

20.2 The repository should not be located in a zone which poses any threat to its security.

20.3 The repository should not be located on ground which is liable to subsidence or on a site which is liable to flooding by natural means, such as underground rivers, or by artificial means, such as water mains.

20.4 The repository should be located on an island site, standing free of neighbouring buildings. If it is not free-standing, it should be capable of being completely protected from dangers posed by neighbouring buildings.

20.5 The repository should be large enough to accommodate current holdings of archives and to offer adequate space for future requirements and expansion in the medium term, that is 20 to 30 years.

20.6 The repository should be accessible to potential users and to cultural and educational institutions.

20.7 The repository should be accessible by road and by public transport.

20.8 The repository should be sited so that it is near to, or easily accessible from, the parent organisation.

21. EXTERNAL AND INTERNAL CONSTRUCTION

21.1 The repository should be of robust construction and provide high thermal inertia, and with adequate protection for all roofs, walls, floors, ceilings, doors and windows against intrusion, fire, flood, damp, excessive sunlight and other weather conditions.

21.2 The repository should include the following accommodation:

- a delivery and reception area for the unloading, initial cleaning and preliminary processing of archives;
- workrooms for processing and exhibition preparation;
- a strongroom or a series of strongrooms where archives are stored;

- a conservation room where archives may be treated;
- offices, a library, a canteen, washrooms and showers for staff;
- a research room where the public may consult archives;
- washroom, locker and refreshment facilities for the public;
- storerooms for packing materials and cleaning equipment

The repository may also include an exhibition room, a lecture theatre and a conference room.

Work area with supervisory windows

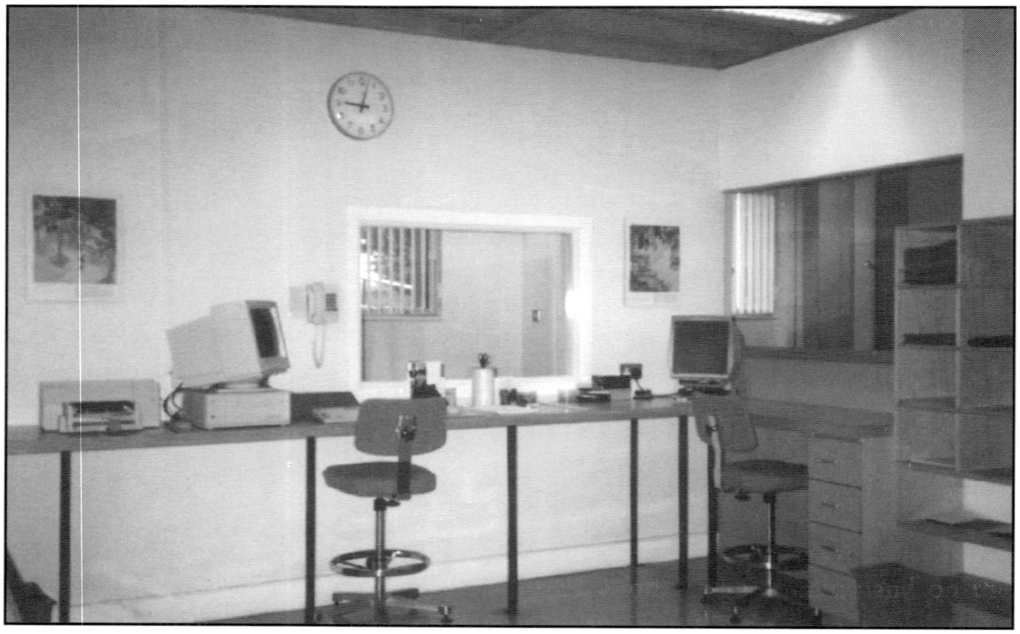

21.3 Plumbing, plant and drains in, above or adjacent to strongrooms should be avoided.

21.4 The construction of floors should be adequate to support the weight of archives to be stored there. The advice of a structural engineer must be sought in relation to the floor loadings. Stronger floors are required for mobile shelving than for static shelving *(see 25.4)*.

21.5 Care should be taken in the choice of finishes applied inside the repository as some may be chemically injurious to archives.

21.6 Provision should be made for the evacuation of water and smoke in an emergency situation.

22. *FIRE PREVENTION*

22.1 Archives are unique and irreplaceable and require the highest standard of protection from fire. These standards are generally more stringent than in other buildings holding large quantities of books or paper and must be rigorously enforced. Fire precautions are designed to reduce to a minimum the possible causes of fire, to detect and extinguish a fire, to ensure the safety of staff and the public and to protect the contents and structure of the repository from damage caused by fire fighting operations.

22.2 In cases where a repository is located in shared premises, it should be separated from other parts of the building by a solid masonry wall, and any doors or covers for other openings should be of four-hour fire resistance. Air-conditioning and ventilation ducts, trunking and conduits which run through shared premises are a particular concern since they aid the spread of fire. The advice of a fire prevention officer should be sought in such instances.

22.3 Fire precautions are subject to legislation and regulation at national and local level. In the Republic of Ireland and in Northern Ireland, the requirements of the respective Departments of the Environment with regard to fire protection must be observed *(see appendix 1)*.

22.4 In all measures concerned with fire prevention, the advice of the local fire authority should be sought.

22.5 The archivist should prepare a disaster plan drawing on the advice of the local fire authority. This should be approved by the archives service's insurers. The local fire brigade should be acquainted with the nature of the repository and its contents in an attempt to keep damage from high-pressure water hoses to a minimum in the event of a fire, but a selective approach by fire fighters cannot be guaranteed.

22.6 During the construction and fitting out of a repository, inflammable finishes and fittings should be kept to a minimum.

22.7 Strongroom doors, ceilings and walls should be of four-hour fire resistance.

22.8 Electrical plant and main switches should be located outside the strongrooms. There should be a master switch outside the repository to control all electrical circuits, except for those providing fire detection and protection.

22.9 Electrical wiring should be checked regularly by a qualified electrician to ensure that it does not present a hazard. In an existing building adapted for use as a repository, electrical wiring should be of recent installation.

22.10 Electrical fittings should be of totally enclosed metal-clad patterns. Cable insulation should be flame-retardant and fluorescent lamp ballast units should be individually fused.

22.11 Good housekeeping is an invaluable aid to fire prevention. The strongrooms should be kept clean and tidy at all times, and loose documents and other combustible material should not be left out of their containers for longer than necessary.

22.12 Naked flames should be prohibited in the repository at all times, even during maintenance work.

22.13 Smoking by members of staff should be confined to one clearly designated area, such as a staff room or canteen.

22.14 The repository should be fitted with smoke alarms linked to a central control unit. Adequate procedures for servicing alarm calls should be established.

22.15 An automatic water or gas-based fire extinguishing system, complying with BS 5306, should be installed. The system should be so designed to detect a fire, sound an alarm, allow a set time for staff to check whether the alarm is genuine and evacuate the premises, and then to release the extinguishing agent.

22.16 Gas based systems containing CFCs are in the course of being phased out and systems likely to cause environmental damage should not be used. Gas systems which are based on carbon dioxide are lethal to personnel inadvertently trapped and therefore necessitate a longer delay before triggering. Where water sprinkler systems are installed, the sprinkler pipes should fill with water only when fire is detected.

22.17 Portable, non-aqueous fire extinguishers, complying with BS 5423, and wall-mounted fire hoses, complying with BS/EN 671, should also be installed.

22.18 The location of fire hydrants adjacent to the repository should be established and the water pressure checked on a regular basis by an officer of the local fire authority.

22.19 The archives staff should know the location of fire-fighting appliances and should be instructed in their use. A fire drill, drawn up in collaboration with the local fire authority, should be practised regularly.

22.20 As cellulose nitrate film is highly inflammable, it must be stored under strict conditions in a separate, self-contained location outside the repository.

22.21 Flammable material, such as chemicals used in cleaning and conservation, should never be stored in the strongrooms.

22.22 Petrol or diesel operated machinery, such as fork-lift trucks, should not be allowed to remain in the strongrooms while not in use.

23. *SECURITY FROM INTRUSION*

23.1 Because of their unique and irreplaceable nature, archives may be attractive to thieves and the repository should be secured against intrusion.

23.2 All external doors to the repository should be fitted with secure locking systems complying with BS 3621. Doors of emergency exit must comply with fire regulations. Doors left open for public access, deliveries or staff use should be monitored at all times.

23.3 For security and environmental control, it is preferable that strongrooms where archives are stored should not be fitted with windows *(see 24.8)*. All windows in the repository vulnerable to intrusion should be secured with bars, grilles, toughened glass, metal roller shutters, intruder sensors, or with a combination of these measures.

23.4 All other means of access to a repository, such as lifts, staircases or ventilation shafts should be secured against unlawful intrusion.

23.5 The repository should be fitted with an intruder alarm system complying with IS 199, which should be connected to a central control unit. Procedures should be put in place for servicing alarm calls.

23.6 In shared premises, internal doors between the repository and other parts of the building should be locked securely when the repository is not occupied.

23.7 Access to the repository and to the strongrooms must be controlled at all times. Absolutely no-one, apart from archives staff, should be allowed into the strongrooms unaccompanied. Maintenance workers must be accompanied and supervised by archives staff at all times.

23.8 Keys to the repository and especially to the strongrooms should be strictly controlled and should only be issued through senior members of repository staff.

23.9 Theft of archives may also occur in the research room *(see section 26 for measures to prevent this).*

24. ENVIRONMENTAL CONTROL

24.1 Archives are highly susceptible to damage and decay arising from storage in an unsuitable environment. If the atmosphere in the strongrooms is too dry or polluted, documents will become brittle; if the atmosphere is too damp, mould will grow on documents; and if the atmosphere is too warm, the chemical structure of documents will start to break down. Light also causes deterioration of archives. In many instances, damage caused by unsuitable storage conditions is irreparable.

24.2 Archives on paper and parchment should be stored at a constant temperature and relative humidity. The temperature and relative humidity levels recommended by BS 5454 are in the range 13°C to 18°C and 55% to 65% respectively. Constant means 24 hours a day, every day of the year. Despite the cost of maintaining a constant stable environment, this is more cost-effective than conservation treatment necessitated by inadequate storage.

24.3 Archives on materials other than paper and parchment require different storage conditions. BS 5454 recommends that the following range is broadly acceptable for the principal records in this category: temperature between 13°C and 16°C; relative humidity between 50% and 60%. For storage of microfilm see 25.6.9. Special and separate microclimates are also required for the safe storage of black and white photographs, colour photographs, video tapes, audio discs, audio cylinders, cinematic film and other media. Specialist advice should be sought as required

24.4 Archives in electronic form require stringent storage conditions to prevent damage and consequent loss of data. Magnetic tapes must be stored at a constant temperature in the range 17°C to 20°C and in constant relative humidity in the range 35% to 45%.

24.5 To ensure maintenance of correct temperature and relative humidity, air-conditioning units should be installed in the strongrooms. To prevent pollution, inlet air drawn from outside should be induced through carbon filters in order to reduce sulphur dioxide and oxides of nitrogen to a concentration not exceeding 10 $\mu g/m^3$.

24.6 Excessive humidity is a common problem, in older buildings and excessive dryness in modern buildings. If air-conditioning cannot be installed, humidification and dehumidification units may be utilised to achieve the required environment. The strongrooms should also be ventilated in accordance with BS 5454.

24.7 The strongrooms must be monitored at all times to ensure that temperature and relative humidity stay within the prescribed ranges. This is best achieved by installing a recording thermohygrograph, which should be calibrated regularly. Manual checking of the environment does not provide a continuous record and is time-consuming and inaccurate. If temperature and relative humidity go outside the prescribed ranges at any time, remedial work must be carried out at once.

24.8 All light is damaging to archives, but the ultra-violet element of sunlight is especially dangerous, as it can cause a breakdown of the chemical composition of paper. Solar heat gain from sunlight can also complicate the task of maintaining prescribed levels of temperature and relative humidity. For these reasons, and on grounds of security *(see 23.3)* there should not be any windows in the strongrooms. Where existing strongrooms are fitted with windows, protective film and blinds should be installed to reduce ultra-violet radiation, solar gain and excessive brightness. Proper precautions should also be taken in the research room to prevent light from damaging archives produced there.

24.9 Pollution caused by dust is a particular hazard in archives, and may affect staff as well as documents. The strongrooms should be vacuumed regularly and all walls, floors and ceilings in the strongrooms should be sealed with fire-resistant sealant. Documents which are being accessioned to the archives should be thoroughly cleaned of surface dirt before being placed in the strongrooms *(see 16.3)*.

25. THE STRONGROOMS

25.1 The strongrooms are intended to provide safe, secure, stable, orderly and permanent accommodation for the archives. Nothing else should be stored there *(see 25.7)*. The area must be fitted out with shelving or other means of storage. The fabric of the building, electrical and plumbing installations, fire prevention and environment are covered in sections 21, 22 and 24.

25.2 The strongrooms must be treated as a high security area. Unauthorised access must be forbidden and maintenance workers must be supervised at all times. If possible, the geography of the building should be designed so as to prevent public access to the strongrooms. If not, doors providing access to the strongrooms should be secured by a locking system which can be opened only by staff.

(left)

Mobile shelving in strongroom, view of main gangway

(right)

Shelves storing boxes

(opposite page left)

Static shelves in strongroom, view of aisle between runs of bays

(right)

Shelves storing boxes

25.3 Management of the strongrooms

25.3.1 Location

The precise location of all archives in the strongrooms should be documented so that access is not dependent on the personal knowledge of an individual.

Every bay of shelving or shelf and every item stored there should be numbered in a simple and logical manner. These numbers should be used for identification in the shelf list and location list. Information technology can be of benefit in automating the production and maintenance of the shelf list and the location list, and also in controlling the movement of the documents.

25.4.5 ARRANGEMENT OF RUNS

The shelving should be arranged in a configuration which makes maximum use of floor space and conforms to regulations for emergency escape and the recommended widths of aisles between rows of shelves and main gangways running at right angles. The recommendations of BS 5454 in these matters are widely applied.

Gangways and aisles:

Main gangways should not measure less than 1100 mm. If pallets or other mechanised trolleys are to be used for moving large quantities of archives, gangways and doors must be sufficiently wide. To facilitate access to contents of shelves, aisles should measure 450 mm + depth of deepest shelf, but not less than a minimum of 900 mm. This principle also applies to other storage units *(see 25.5.1 -2)*.

Length of runs of shelving:

Runs should not exceed 10m in length.

25.4.6 PLACEMENT OF SHELVING WITHIN THE STRONGROOMS.

Shelving must not be placed under water pipes, against outside walls or windows, or against radiators. If possible, internal walls should be avoided because problems, such as leaks, could go undetected.

25.4.7 SHELVING FOR LARGE ROLLS

Archives too large to be stored flat should be rolled and stored on shelves supporting their entire length. This may mean placing them parallel to the aisle. If rolls are wrapped or bagged *(see 25.6.7)*, they should be stored on a narrow shelf designed to prevent them moving backwards or forwards. If rolls are boxed, shelving of standard depth may be used. The shelving should be designed without vertical uprights on the aisle side to facilitate removal and replacement of long items. In other respects the shelving should conform to the description given in 25.4.3 - 6 above.

25.5 OTHER EQUIPMENT

25.5.1 PLAN CABINETS

Plan cabinets should be made from non-combustible material, preferably steel finished with enamel conforming to BS 826; be well finished with no rough edges or spots; drawers should move along their shorter side on ball bearing slides and should operate smoothly when fully loaded; drawers should be fitted with a safety stop to prevent accidental removal, with a hinged retaining bar at the front and a solid hood at least 150 mm deep at the back; drawers should not be deeper than 45 mm; units of drawers

(left)
Microfilm storage cabinets

(right)
Shelves storing large volumes and plan cabinets

should be capable of being permanently bolted together, to a maximum height of 1750 mm; there should be a plinth of at least 100 mm on each unit; drawers should be fitted with label holders.

25.5.2 CABINETS FOR MICROFILM AND ELECTRONIC RECORDS

Roll microfilm and microfiche should be stored in drawers in steel cabinets made for this purpose; for environment, packing and storage see 25.6.9. Electronic records should be stored in metal cabinets; for environment see 24.4 and for packing and storage see 25.6.10.

25.5.3 EQUIPMENT FOR MOVING ARCHIVES

Trolleys and hand trucks are required to assist in the movement of archives around the building. These should be of sound construction, large enough to carry the documents, well finished and free from protuberances, have rubber wheels, easily manoeuvred and be compatible with the principle of not causing damage to the archives.

25.6 PACKING & STORAGE

25.6.1 PACKING ARCHIVES FOR PERMANENT STORAGE

As far as possible archives should be packed inside archival quality rigid containers or wrapping, and placed in order on shelves. The use of containers or wrapping minimises the damage caused by air, dust, light and friction

Selection of archival quality packing material

against other documents, facilitates routine housekeeping and helps to protect in a disaster situation, such as fire or flood. Careful consideration should be given to the choice of packing and storage. The smallest container into which the documents fit flat should always be used, and containers should be filled to the top but not overfilled. Many documents will require enclosure in folders or envelopes before boxing. Folders and envelopes are themselves quite bulky and a reasonable number of sheets should be placed in each. Transparent polyester packing must not be used on documents that have not been treated by a conservator *(see section 28).*

25.6.2 BOXES AND OTHER PACKING MATERIALS

The optimum size of box depends on size of the contents and the shelving on which it will be placed: it should be large enough to accommodate the documents comfortably and to allow their removal without damage or difficulty. It may be necessary to have several sizes. Other packing materials will also be required: folders, envelopes, wrapping paper, tissue paper, tubes, cotton tape and labels.

25.6.3 ARCHIVAL QUALITY

Boxes and all other materials which are in direct contact with archives intended for long term preservation should be of archival quality. Manufacturers' claims in this regard should be checked. Archival quality materials are acid-free and are treated to provide a positive environment for the documents thus contributing to their preservation. Non-archival quality materials actively damage documents. Archival quality materials are expensive but labour costs are also high and when proper materials are used, the archivist can be sure that the work is complete and will not have to be redone in the future. Where it is not possible to purchase all materials of this quality, at least a percentage of those purchased every year should be archival quality. Some archives, such as photographs, require special grade archival quality packing materials.

25.6.4 STORING LOOSE DOCUMENTS AND FILES

Loose documents and files should be packed in boxes and stored flat. Loose papers should be enclosed in folders or envelopes, and files may need re-foldering before boxing.

25.6.5 STORING VOLUMES

The best storage of bound volumes will depend on their size and condition. Bound volumes are designed to stand vertically on shelves, but if they are oversized, that is a height is greater than 400 mm and thickness greater than 100 mm, or damaged, they should be stored horizontally. In vertical storage, care should be taken that volumes support one another without undue pressure, and that removal and replacement are possible; similar sized volumes should be stored together to avoid distortion of bindings; vertical supports the full size of the volumes should be provided as necessary. Large, heavy or damaged volumes should be stored horizontally, and shelving should be adjusted so that they are stacked only one or two volumes high.

Volumes should always be boxed or wrapped and the choice will depend on the availability of a suitable box. Care should be taken that volumes stored vertically in boxes are well supported, if necessary by placing extra packing in the box. Small volumes may be stored horizontally in boxes.

25.6.6 STORING OUTSIZE DOCUMENTS: FLAT

Flat maps, plans and documents up to AO size should be stored in folders placed in large flat boxes or horizontal plan cabinets. They should **never** be stored in vertical hanging cabinets.

25.6.7 STORING OUTSIZE DOCUMENTS: ROLLED

Documents larger than AO size should be rolled around cores approximately 100 mm in diameter and wrapped, bagged or boxed. They should be stored on shelves supporting their entire length, parallel to the aisle. Rolled archives should never be placed inside tubes.

25.6.8 STORING PHOTOGRAPHS

Photographic archives consist of materials that are very diverse and they all require storage in archival quality materials manufactured specifically for this purpose. The items themselves may be of varying chemical stability and it is advisable that they be stored singly in a special quality envelope or folder. Prints and negatives should be stored separately from each other for security. Folders or envelopes containing prints and negatives should be placed flat in special archival quality boxes. Plastic materials should not be used on most photographic materials, unless advised by a photographic conservator. Glass plate negatives should be wrapped in paper or placed in envelopes and stored vertically supporting each other in special archival quality boxes.

25.6.9 Storing microfilms

Film is very sensitive to environmental conditions. The storage recommendations for microfilm depend on the film base concerned and whether the film is a master/storage copy or a work copy. The two copies should always be distinguished and stored separately, as should film on separate bases. Film intended for master/storage copy purposes should meet the storage requirements of ANSI/NAPM IT9.11-1993 and the packing requirements of ANSI IT9.2-1991. Working copies of film should be placed in inert plastic containers or special quality boxes (except acetate film which should not be stored in paper). The boxes should be placed in drawers in steel cabinets made for this purpose.

25.6.10 Storing electronic records

The information contained on floppy disks should be transferred to a more stable storage medium. Computer tapes should be enclosed in inert plastic or metal containers and stored vertically on metal shelves. To guard against data loss, a statistical sample of all tapes should be tested annually. Adequate technical information must be maintained for each file..

25.6.11 Storing cellulose nitrate film

Film made on a cellulose nitrate base is inherently unstable and a fire risk and should not be stored in the same strongroom as other archives. It should be copied on to a modern stable film base, but if this is not possible, it should be stored in metal containers in a cool, well ventilated and dry area and in a place where it does not cause a risk. This film was widely used until 1939 and occasionally until the mid-1950s. It is known to have been used for microfilming and as a support base for photographs.

25.6.12 Other specialised storage

Video tapes, audio discs, audio cylinders, cinematic film and other specialised media all need special storage and specific advice should be sought as the problems arise.

25.7 Store rooms

Separate store rooms should be provided for packing materials and cleaning equipment and materials. These items should not be stored in the strong rooms. Packing materials, especially boxes, can take up large amounts of space. Cleaning materials may be hazardous to archives.

26. *THE RESEARCH ROOM AND ITS ADMINISTRATION*

26.1 Protection of archives requires stringent security provisions relating to access to and use of the research room.

26.2 The research room provides a safe and secure space for researchers to inspect documents, space for finding aids and other reference material and space for staff. The design, layout and operation of the research room require careful thought about the functions which it is intended to fulfil and this depends on the space available, the number of documents to be consulted and the number of researchers to be catered for. The primary task of staff working in the research room is to assist researchers' queries and to invigilate. Any other work assigned should be closely defined.

(left)
View of a small reading room

(right)
View of a reading room showing finding aids and reference books

26.3 ACCOMMODATION

26.3.1 Researchers must be provided with a seat and a table at which to read documents. Many archives use large tables seating several researchers, but the divisions between researchers should be clear. The size of the reading tables will be determined by the amount of space available and the type of documents to be consulted, but for most purposes, a table 1000 mm wide by 900 mm deep is sufficient. The exception is for the consultation of maps or other outsize documents where larger tables will be required. Tables must be made of materials that will not cause damage to the archives, have a smooth finish and be free of protuberances and obstructions. Table lights obstruct the use of large documents and can be a hindrance to invigilation. Power points should be provided for researchers using electric or electronic equipment.

26.3.2 Finding aids usually consist of lists in book form, card indexes in drawers and microfiche readers. There may also be computer facilities for on-line access. Shelves for finding aids, and counter or table space for convenient consultation, should be provided.

26.3.3 Staff must have a desk from which to answer enquiries, deal with paper-work, answer the telephone and supervise the researchers.

26.3.4 There should be good natural light, but sunlight must not fall directly on to documents. Fluorescent lighting giving light levels at table level of 50 lux should be installed, and fluorescent tubes should be fitted with UV filters to eliminate light waves under 400 nm. Windows should be fitted with blinds to help control excessive brightness.

26.4 OPERATION OF THE RESEARCH ROOM

26.4.1 The research room must be invigilated at all times. It is an essential part of the archives' guarantee of the authenticity and integrity of the holdings that unsupervised access is never allowed. This is particularly difficulty in a small archives service, and will of necessity mean closing at lunch time, and may mean opening only at fixed times or by appointment. The installation of Closed Circuit Television may be considered an aid where only a small number of staff is available; it is relatively inexpensive, but requires careful specification and operational procedures.

26.4.2 The security of the documents requires that strict control be kept over their inspection by public and staff. This is achieved by means of systems to control the researchers and systems to track the documents *(see 25.3.2)*.

26.4.3 The control of researchers requires that all researchers have a researcher's ticket; records of issue of tickets are kept; all researchers are subject to a standard set of rules; a daily attendance book is kept. A permanent record of each researcher must be kept, including name and address, research interests and, where relevant, institution to which attached.

26.4.4 Control of documents requires that a record is kept of all documents removed from the strongrooms, whether for consultation by the public or for staff use, with a proper audit trail; the number of documents produced to a researcher at any one time should be limited *(see 25.3.1-2)*.

26.4.5 Researchers should be informed by leaflet or video presentation of the document handling and consultation regulations which apply in the research room. These should be strictly enforced by staff at all times.

26.4.6 The research room should provide reference books relating to holdings; information leaflets on the holdings and services available. A strictly controlled photocopying service, and other forms of reprography where appropriate may be provided *(see section 27)*.

26.4.7 Information technology has many uses in the administration of the research room: to store information about researchers; to keep detailed records of documents issued and returned; to compile statistics of researchers and of documents issued; to provide a breakdown of documents consulted; to facilitate correspondence and replies to enquiries. Most of these functions will be facilitated by the use of information technology but the procedures must already have been designed in accordance with the principles of archival management of the research room. The archivist must be involved in the choice of information technology in order to ensure that the basic requirements are met and that archival administration is not curtailed by technical limitations.

Technical Services

27. *REPROGRAPHY*

27.1 Reprography is an essential service, both internally to the archives itself and to researchers and parent bodies. Archives can require reprography for many reasons: reference copies for researchers, legal copies, security, preservation, publication, acquisition, administration, publicity and space saving.

27.2 Serious attention must be given to reproduction rights and copyright as it is more difficult to retain control in these matters when copies of documents are provided. Permission to publish documents must be requested before publication.

27.3 In some cases, the reproduction of archives is subject to legal provisions. The archivist must be fully aware of the legal implications of reproducing archives under such circumstances.

27.4 In setting up a reprographic service each archives will have different requirements but the following basic considerations should apply: identify the objectives of the service and the needs of the main users, for example, security copies or copies for researchers; decide which type of copy is most appropriate, such as microfilm or electrostatic copy; find suitable space in the building; provide staff to operate the system; plan funding for initial costs, running costs and maintenance and replacement; plan organisation and management; decide what charges are to be made to users; examine if objectives are best met by contracting out all or part of the service.

27.5 Archives should be aware of the dangers and disadvantages of reprography: physical damage through handling; chemical damage through exposure to intense light; loss of control of reproduction rights and copyright; large financial investment and commitment of staff. Archives have reprography requirements different from those of other users of this technology and care should be taken when choosing a system.

27.6 The reprographic policy of the archives should be defined, be openly stated and consistently applied. Decisions should be made at policy level about which documents to reproduce and how, in accordance with the archives service's preservation policy *(see sections 9 and 11)*. Damage to documents is a major consideration and many archives services impose restrictions on vulnerable items, such as bound books or large documents. The policy should also consider matters such as how to minimise damage to frequently copied documents.

27.7 Accommodation for the reprographic service must be provided within the building. Photographic or film processing must take place in a separate room, because of the dangers from chemicals. If possible, other reprographic activities should also be housed in a separate room. If this is not possible, the service should be accommodated in an area serving a compatible function, but must never be situated in the strongrooms. In general, this is to ensure that orderly procedures are maintained, but there are also technical reasons, such as a rise in light levels caused by microfilming or photography and the production of ozone by electrostatic copiers. Good ventilation is essential in a reprographic room.

27.8 The reprographic service must be properly organised and managed. Staff should be trained in the operation of the machinery, the handling of the documents and the keeping of good order in the reprographic room. The same level of control should be required for documents sent for reprography as for documents produced for the research room. There should be no danger of documents losing their identification or getting mixed up with others. The room should be cleaned regularly. Documents should not be left overnight in the reprographic room.

27.9 MAIN OPTIONS IN REPROGRAPHY

27.9.1 ELECTROSTATIC COPIERS

Electrostatic copiers or photocopiers are the most commonly available form of reprography and are quick, convenient and easily provided in-house. Nevertheless, it should be noted that electrostatic copying is one of the most damaging forms of document reproduction. Some archives services now actively discourage this method of reproduction in the interests of preservation.

Care should be taken when choosing a copier to ensure that the platen is large enough for most uses, that the cover can be removed and when removed there are no projections likely to cause damage. Copiers with platens that move or that require automatic feeding of the document should be avoided.

27.9.2 MICROFILM AND OTHER MICROFORMS

Microforms are reduced photographic images of documents, requiring magnification in order to be read.There are many different microforms, but the most common are roll microfilm and microfiche. There are also micro-opaques, updateable microfiche, microfilm jackets, aperture cards and COM (computer output on microfilm). Microforms have many advantages: they are compact, durable, relatively cheap, convenient and easy to use; easy to duplicate for publication or multiple users; can be quicker to consult than the documents and contribute to the preservation of the originals by saving wear and tear. Microforms also have disadvantages: microfilming to archival standards is more expensive than commercial microfilming; it requires good preparatory work before filming and adherence to strict technical standards; it requires special machinery for viewing and printing, some of which is extremely expensive; not all documents are suitable for microfilming; users are somewhat resistant to microforms as they lose contact with the original documents and many find reading microforms tiring or uncomfortable. The choice of microform will be determined by the overall policy of the archives.

27.9.2.1 Microfilm for archival purposes must be manufactured, processed and stored in accordance with recognised standards *(see appendix 1)*. Provision must be made for the separate storage of the master negatives in environmentally controlled conditions *(see 25.6.9)*.

27.9.2.2 Preparation of archives for microfilming is essential to the usefulness of the finished film. Archives must be arranged, numbered and listed in the normal manner before filming, and the finding aids through which the microforms will be accessed must be thought out in advance *(see section 17)*.

27.9.2.3 Microfilming requires considerable investment in technology and staff and many organisations contract this function out. Agreements must be made in advance with contractors covering the technical standards and the organisation of the work. It is preferable for security that the filming be carried out in the archives premises. If the documents must be removed, stringent conditions should be attached to the contract regarding carriage, security, handling and duration of filming. Sample films should be obtained from the contractor at an early stage in the filming. All films and documents should be examined upon return.

27.9.2.4 Microform readers must be provided for users.

27.9.3 PHOTOGRAPHY

Because of the expense and skill required, only the largest archives offer in-house photographic services. However, photographs are often requested, especially of visually attractive documents or photographic archives. A professional photographer should be engaged as required to do this work. Users are sometimes allowed to take their own photographs or videos, with or without lighting, and this should be strictly controlled and supervised.

27.9.3.1 Photography presents several dangers to archives, especially when carried out in an outside studio: high levels of light for prolonged periods, manipulation of archives into positions convenient to the photographer, chemicals likely to be present in a studio and activities incompatible with security (smoking, eating etc). Documents should be kept in the studio for the minimum time, and never overnight, and they should be under the constant supervision of a member of the archives staff. Old photographic archives are particularly vulnerable.

27.9.3.2 Documentation should be kept showing what photographs have been taken, in what format and if possible the negatives should be kept by the archives.

27.9.4 DIGITAL IMAGING

The technology of digital imaging has become increasingly accessible in recent times. The image of a textual or graphic document is captured on a laser scanner and stored on computer, and can be viewed or reproduced. It is especially useful for graphic documents. This is a relatively new process, and while it hold promise for use in archives, many new developments are expected over the next few years. Like microfilming, digital imaging requires selection, intellectual control and high technical standards.

28. *CONSERVATION*

28.1 Conservation treatment of archives should be carried out in the context of the preservation policy of the archives service *(see sections 9 and 11)*. A preservation policy has two elements: preventive conservation which aims to avoid or minimise damage to archives, and the provision of conservation treatment for archives that are damaged.

28.2 The archivist must be in overall charge of all conservation policy and activity, from the simplest handling and packing to work in the conservation workshop.

28.3 The best policy is always to concentrate on prevention by providing a sound and secure building *(see sections 19 - 21)*, protected from fire hazards *(see section 22)*, suitable environment *(see section 24)*, high quality packing and storage *(see section 25)*, good practice in handling and use by staff and researchers and enforcement of the policy regarding reproduction *(see sections 26 - 27)*.

28.4 All preservation and conservation decisions should be guided by the principle that nothing should be done that cannot be reversed or that will cause harm to the documents. If there is any doubt about the long term effects of a process, it should be avoided. BS 4971 sets out standards for conservation repair and binding.

28.5 A conservation workshop where damaged documents are repaired and treated is an important part of this preservation and conservation policy and activity.

28.6 Conservation is a skilled and specialist profession in its own right and repair or interference with the physical fabric of documents should never be undertaken by untrained persons.

28.7 Conservation work can be costly, and proposals should be evaluated carefully and the following questions considered: the archival value of the documents; their place in the scale of priorities; their packing and storage after conservation; their use by researchers; whether alternative formats should be used. Where there are limited funds, it should be considered how the best value can be obtained from the amount available.

28.8 Complete records of all conservation work must be kept, including a record of processes and substances used, dates and names of conservators. This is part of the archives service's guarantee of the integrity and authenticity of the archives. This documentation is required whether the work is carried out within the archives service or on an outside contract. Records of work carried out can be kept manually or on computer.

28.9 A conservation survey is useful in order to define the conservation priorities and the overall conservation needs of the archives service. This should be carried out by a professional conservator in conjunction with the archivist.

28.10 IN-HOUSE CONSERVATION WORKSHOP

28.10.1 All archives hold or accession archives which require conservation repair and provision can be made for this by establishing an in-house conservation workshop. It is essential that conservation activities are in accordance with the overall aims, management structure and preservation policy of the archives service, and that the relationships between archival and conservation staff are defined.

28.10.2 Setting up a conservation workshop represents a serious commitment on the part of any organisation in terms of funding, staffing and operation. It requires a policy definition of the role of the workshop in the administration of the archives service, accommodation, staff and funding for establishment and running costs.

28.10.3 When setting up a conservation workshop, advice should be sought from a consultant. Major expenditure is involved in the fitting out of a workshop and the purchase of equipment. The cost of a consultant is a good investment if it avoids expensive mistakes. There are many different kinds of deterioration or damage to archives and many different solutions, and expert advice may be helpful in deciding an area of major specialisation. None but the largest workshops could hope to cover the full range of conservation repair.

28.10.4 Accommodation for a workshop must consist of a suitable and separate room. Heavy machinery will require strong floor loadings. Conformity with health and safety regulations and fire regulations is mandatory. Depending on the processes to be carried out and the chemicals to be used, matters governed by these regulations, such as escape in an emergency and the venting of fumes, must be considered at an early stage in the design. Separate secure storage for chemicals is likely to be required.

28.10.5 A workshop should be headed by a trained professional conservator. Many workshops engage trainees or newly trained conservators, but they should work under the direct supervision of the conservator.

28.11 The conservator, whether employed by the institution or on outside contract, must be answerable to the archivist and must work in conjunction with the archivist to further the preservation policy of the archives service.

28.12 CONTRACTING OUT

Even archives services with a conservation workshop may sometimes need specialist work to be executed outside. Because there are more risks involved than with in-house treatment, certain precautions should be taken. A thorough examination of the documents concerned must be carried out in advance by the archives service, and a record must be kept of their condition, format and special features. A written description of the proposed treatment must be provided by the conservator. The archives service must be satisfied about the security and safety of the documents during the work by carrying out an inspection of the premises. A proper contract should be drawn up with the conservator including matters such as carriage, insurance, security, handling and duration of the work. A complete report describing the work done must be supplied by the conservator when the work is completed.

28.13 Cooperation with other organisations in conservation may be a solution for some archives services.

Records Management

29. *FUNCTIONS OF THE ARCHIVIST*

29.1 BASIC CONCEPTS

29.1.1 Records have a life-span divided into three stages: current, non-current and archival. Their process of ageing is referred to as the `life-cycle of records' and this concept is based on the usefulness of records from the moment of their creation until their disposition by retention or disposal.

29.2 FUNCTIONS OF THE ARCHIVIST & RECORDS MANAGEMENT STAFF

29.2.1 While a records management programme provides quantifiable benefits to administration in the creation, use, storage and retrieval of information, its aim must also be to identify records which are to be permanently preserved as archives. Because of this, the archivist is the person most qualified to provide a records management service to administration.

29.2.2 The records management functions of the archivist range from the design of record-keeping systems within an administration, through prescribing record formats, to control of the processes for their disposition, either by destruction or by permanent preservation as archives *(see section 15)*.

29.2.3 The archivist publicises the records management programme to those responsible for the formulation of policy in the organisation, alerts them to its administrative and archival benefits and demonstrates their role in the achievement of the programme.

29.2.4 The position of the archivist within the management structure of the parent organisation should be such as to give authority and effect to the records management policy which it is required to formulate and implement.

29.2.5 The archivist is responsible for ensuring that all personnel involved in records management functions receive adequate training, either from the archivist or from external sources.

29.2.6 It is the function of records centre staff to manage the records created by the organisation to which it is attached in accordance with the records management policy formulated by the archivist. This will require staff to become involved in activities ranging from the creation and design of record-keeping systems for administration, through to the operation of a records service. Staff must be familiar with the administrative structure of the record creating agency, be aware of where records are generated and in what format, and appreciate their administrative and informational value. Staff should also actively acquire documentation and other records which, though not generated by the parent organisation, contain information on its activities, such as publications, newspaper articles, printed reports, and even the private papers of members of staff.

29.3 OBJECTIVES OF THE RECORDS MANAGEMENT PROGRAMME

29.3.1 Records management must serve the needs of both administration and archives. A records management programme attempts to guarantee that an administration has control over all its documents as early in their life-cycle as possible. From an archival perspective, records management ensures that records worthy of permanent preservation as archives are identified at the earliest possible moment, that arrangements are made for their preservation once their use within the parent organisation has ceased, and that they are stored under suitable conditions pending transfer to the archives.

29.3.2 BENEFITS TO ADMINISTRATION

The records management programme ensures that records are created in an organised manner, in a manageable quantity and in a suitable format. It allows records to remain in offices only as long as they are in active use and prescribes procedures for the storage and disposition of non-current records.

29.3.3 Records management offers savings in the storage of records by providing for retention of only those records which must be kept to comply with legal requirements or to answer informational needs and by identifying records for destruction at the earliest possible stage in their life-cycle.

29.3.4 The records management programme is designed to achieve ease of retrieval of records required for administrative purposes during non-currency.

29.3.5 The records management programme facilitates speed of retrieval of records, effecting savings in operational costs.

29.3.6 Security of records and the information they contain is a source of anxiety for every organisation. Information is a major asset and its loss, either through theft or disaster, can seriously undermine the functioning of the organisation. The records management programme should, in addition to providing for the secure storage of records, identify vital records which are indispensable to the organisation and makes provision for their protection *(see 29.4.8)*.

29.3.7 BENEFITS TO ARCHIVES

A records management programme should be designed to facilitate the selection of certain records for permanent preservation as archives in conformity with the appraisal strategies of the archivist.

29.3.8 A records management programme ensures that records worthy of permanent preservation as archives are created, maintained and preserved in an appropriate physical form. For example, records such as minute books may need to be preserved in original hard-copy rather than in microfilm and permanent paper should be used for such records. It is imperative that the archivist is involved at the earliest possible stage in the creation of electronic records to identify those which should be preserved permanently and to ensure they are accompanied by adequate documentation and metadata and preserved in the most accessible and appropriate form.

29.3.9 A records management programme ensures that records are deposited in the archives in a regular and organised fashion according to procedures laid down by the archivist.

29.4 IMPLEMENTATION OF THE RECORDS MANAGEMENT PROGRAMME

The records management programme ensures intervention from the point of creation and design of the record-keeping system and includes the following procedures:

- surveying of records
- transfer of records to the records centre
- appraisal of records
- disposition of records
- protection of vital records

29.4.1 SURVEYING OF RECORDS

The starting point of a records management programme should be a survey of records within administration, covering both current and non-current records. Its purpose is to establish the function and administrative structure of the organisation and to assess its informational needs. It should examine current records systems: how records are created, and maintained; how and by whom the records are used; the number of record series and their inter-relationship, format and condition. The survey is used to provide the archivist with the information necessary to determine the resources required and to design records management systems.

29.4.2 TRANSFER OF RECORDS TO THE RECORDS CENTRE

Procedures for the transfer of records to the records centre should be outlined in a manual of guidelines prepared by the archivist. These guidelines should provide staff of the record creating agency with practical instructions for the execution of record transfers: the physical preparation of records, the preparation of transfer lists and the transport of records.

29.4.3 APPRAISAL OF RECORDS

Records transferred to the records centre must not be allowed to remain there indefinitely. Some may require appraisal by an archivist to assess their evidential and informational value and to decide on disposition; others may be disposed of in accordance with a schedule or list of records.

29.4.4 DISPOSITION OF RECORDS

The disposition function of the records management programme should be controlled by means of a schedule. The schedule should be drawn up from information obtained from the records survey.

29.4.5 The schedule should prescribe lengths of currency and non-currency for all records, together with disposition arrangements. The schedule should include details of those records which need to be appraised by the archivist.

29.4.6 The schedule should be widely circulated within the record creating agency and must have the approval of management.

29.4.7 The schedule must be regularly reviewed and updated as necessary.

29.4.8 PROTECTION OF VITAL RECORDS

Every records management programme should make provision for the protection of records containing information vital to the functioning of the organisation. Vital records are those records required to reconstruct the legal, financial and operational basis of an organisation in a disaster situation and allow it to continue functioning. The records management programme identifies vital records and ensures that copies are made and stored in a secure location so that administration can have continued access to information in the event of a disaster where damage is sustained by original records.

30. THE RECORDS CENTRE

30.1 ROLE OF THE RECORDS CENTRE

30.1.1 The records centre is a building which provides cost-effective and secure accommodation for the temporary storage of non-current records, most of which will not be permanently preserved.

30.1.2 The existence of the records centre facilitates the orderly removal of non-current records from valuable space within the administrative offices of the creating agency to cheaper accommodation.

30.1.3 The records centre should retain all non-current records only as long as prescribed by the records schedule. No records should remain in the records centre indefinitely or permanently.

30.1.4 Overall responsibility for the administration of the records centre belongs to the archivist, although the routine tasks associated with the flow of records through the centre can be performed by other staff according to guidelines provided by the archivist *(see 31.5)*.

30.1.5 Records in the records centre remain the property of the creating agency and their confidentiality and security is assured.

30.1.6 Records in the records centre must be accessible to the creating agency. This will entail the provision of a records retrieval service.

30.2 THE BUILDING

30.2.1 A records centre may be a purpose-built or an adapted building. The archivist must be consulted at all stages of the project from site selection to the finished records centre.

30.2.2 A records centre can usually be housed in a warehouse structure, which should be secure, clean and capable of housing large quantities of non-current records stored on high density shelving. In the case of a multi-storied building, the advice of a structural engineer should be sought as to the floor-loading capacity of the building.

30.2.3 The records centre building may be shared with another organisation whose use of the building is for a similar purpose, provided that internal accommodation strictly segregates the space allocated to each.

30.2.4 In the case of a small organisation, the use of commercial records storage for non-current records may be a viable option. If commercial records storage is to be used, the standard of accommodation should be on a par with that available in a records centre administered as part of an archives service in respect of security, confidentiality, storage and packing, and the professional experience and expertise of staff. Any such proposal should be carefully evaluated.

30.2.5 Regardless of whether the records centre is purpose-built, adapted or shared, or whether recourse is had to a commercial facility, the archivist must ensure that all requirements of the building regulations are observed.

30.3 LOCATION OF THE RECORDS CENTRE

30.3.1 The records centre does not have to be situated in close proximity to the record creating agency or the archives service, but can be located in an area where the cost of accommodation is lower.

30.3.2 However, the records centre must be easily accessible both for the purpose of transferring records and to facilitate records centre staff and services.

30.3.3 The records centre should not be located on ground which is liable to subsidence.

30.3.4 The records centre should not be located on a site liable to flooding either by natural or artificial means.

30.3.5 The records centre should be free-standing or at least be capable of being protected from the dangers caused by neighbouring structures.

30.4 CONSTRUCTION

30.4.1 The records centre should be of solid construction, with adequate protection for all roofs, walls, floors, ceilings doors and windows against fire, flood, damp, excessive sunlight and intrusion.

30.4.2 Accommodation in the records centre should include separate areas for the following: reception and despatch of records; storage of records and appraisal of records. It should also include accommodation for staff and related services which conform to recognised standards.

30.4.3 Plumbing, plant and drains in, above or adjacent to the storage areas should be avoided.

30.4.4 The floors must be capable of supporting the weight of the records stored there. The advice of a structural engineer must be sought.

30.5 SECURITY FROM FIRE

30.5.1 The precautions adopted in an archives repository to guard against fire should also be observed in a records centre *(see section 22)*.

30.6 SECURITY FROM THEFT

30.6.1 The records transferred to the records centre remain the property of the parent organisation and should be kept secure from theft or unauthorised access.

30.6.2 All external access points to the records centre should be fitted with secure doors or other coverings and should be fitted with intruder alarms which are connected to a central control unit and which are monitored and responded to.

30.6.3 Access to the storage areas should be controlled at all times. It is useful to have the administrative offices of the records centre sited at the most convenient point of access to the building.

30.6.4 In a shared facility, internal access points between the various areas allocated to different organisations should be avoided.

30.7 INTERNAL ACCOMMODATION

30.7.1 Every effort should be made to maximise the use of space within the records centre through the use of high density shelving.

30.7.2 The type of shelving chosen for installation will depend on the requirements of the organisation, the configuration of the building and on the advice received from a structural engineer as to the floor loading capacity.

30.7.3 Space should be allowed between the runs of shelving to provide access to the records. The recommendations of BS 5454 are a useful guide in this matter. This space may also have to be wide enough to allow the use of fork-lift trucks for the transport of records.

30.7.4 Occasionally, records centres may have air-conditioned strongrooms for the storage of electronic and microfilm records and security vaults for the storage of confidential, classified or even vital records.

30.8 PACKING

30.8.1 Storage of records in archival quality boxes is not necessary, however, use must be made of containers for storage. These serve to keep the records in order, allow stacking on shelves and facilitate retrieval of records. Boxes must carry a label with an indication of contents by reference number and a location reference.

31. ADMINISTRATION OF THE RECORDS CENTRE

31.1 The archivist is responsible for the administration and budgeting of the records centre.

31.2 The archivist negotiates the necessary agreements and principles for the transfer of non-current records with the relevant divisions of the parent organisation.

31.3 The archivist is responsible for the creation of schedules *(see 29.4.4 - 7).*

31.4 The archivist is responsible for the design and development of the records centre's finding aids and housekeeping records.

31.5 The archivist draws up a manual of guidelines for the operation of the records centre. These guidelines must provide administrative staff with clear and practical instructions for the transfer of records to the centre: the preparation of records and transfer lists, and the method of carriage; must detail for records centre staff the procedures for the transfer to the archives of records intended for permanent preservation and for the disposal of records; must detail the procedure for the authorised retrieval of records. The guidelines must be regularly reviewed and updated as necessary.

31.6 The day-to-day running of the records centre should usually be delegated to support staff acting under the direction of the archivist and operating in accordance with the guidelines provided by the archivist.

31.7 The size of the parent organisation and the volume of records generated will determine the number of records centre staff. Regardless of size, the staffing structure should include a records centre assistant grade. The services of at least one paper-keeper/porter will also be required.

31.8 Records centre staff accept all records transferred to the centre under the records management programme devised by the archivist. They should liaise with the parent organisation in arranging the transfer of non-current records, perform the associated clerical tasks, such as checking of transferred records against the transfer lists, and should maintain adequate information on all non-current records transferred. Such information may be maintained in electronic format.

31.9 Records centre staff maintain all indexes, finding aids and housekeeping records developed by the archivist. These must include information on the physical location of all such records within the centre.

31.10 Records centre staff deal with authorised enquiries from the parent organisation concerning non-current record and provide it with an authorised record retrieval service. They must adequately document all such activities

31.11 Records centre staff must provide a records retrieval service to administration.

31.12 Records centre staff must identify records for transfer to the archives or for destruction in accordance with the provisions of the records management programme.

31.13 Records centre staff should make arrangements for the transfer of records to the archives, or for the destruction of records in accordance with the provisions of the guidelines provided by the archivist.

Services to Private Depositors

32. DEPOSIT AGREEMENTS

32.1 The deposit of collections is a matter of free will by private individuals and private organisations. It is essential that an archives service enters into deposit agreements with depositors, however, deposit of small collections may be accepted by an exchange of letters.

32.2 The deposit agreement should be negotiated between the archivist and the depositor. It should protect the interests of the depositors and of the archives service and outline the responsibilities of both parties.

32.3 In negotiating deposit agreements, the archivist should ensure that depositors clearly understand their implications, scope and potential and are made aware of their responsibilities and those of the archives service.

32.4 In entering into deposit agreements, depositors and the archivist are entitled to negotiate terms of deposit with reference to all matters affecting deposited collections including preservation, conservation, use, access, reproduction, publication, copyright, display, appraisal, processing and security.

32.5 The terms of deposit will define the nature of deposits as either permanent, indefinite or for a fixed period to facilitate the interests both of depositors and the archives service.

32.6 The deposit agreement should be recorded in the form of a contract which clearly states the terms agreed by both parties and outlines their responsibilities. It should be signed by both parties or by their representatives.

32.7 The archives service will enforce the terms of deposit agreed with depositors.

32.8 Many archives services may be in possession of collections which were deposited in the past without the provision of deposit agreements. In the absence of deposit agreements the archives service must act in the best interests of the depositors and apply the highest professional standards to the collections in question.

32.9 If a collection has been deposited without the provision of a deposit agreement, such an agreement may be negotiated by the archivist and the depositor at a later stage.

32.10 If a collection has been deposited without the provision of a deposit agreement, and the negotiation of one is not feasible, the archives service should preserve that collection permanently and should not sell the collection or disperse it, and should only in exceptional circumstances transfer it into the custody of a more appropriate organisation.

33. *PROTECTION OF DEPOSITORS' INTERESTS*

33.1 In accepting a custodial role for deposited collections, the archives service must protect the interests of the depositor by applying the highest professional standards.

33.2 Deposited collections must be stored under conditions compatible with their permanent preservation.

33.3 Deposited collections must be fully processed before being made available to the public.

33.4 The security of deposited collections requires the provision of sufficient detail in descriptive lists, the comprehensive numbering and sub-numbering of documents, the supervision of researchers using documents and the provision of security microfilm.

33.5 The existence of sensitive and confidential information in deposited collections, or the existence of documents covered by legislation, must be identified by the archivist in processing collections and appropriate measures taken to protect them, including clear statements of closure or restrictions in descriptive lists, flash indicators on computerised finding aids and warning labels on boxes and file covers.

33.6 Documents in deposited collections must be physically protected through the imposition of controls by the archivist over their storage, handling, use, reproduction, display and conservation.

34. *ACKNOWLEDGMENT AND GOODWILL*

34.1 The archives service must ensure that the deposit of collections is acknowledged publicly in annual reports and in writing.

34.2 The source of the deposit and the name of the depositor must be recorded in the descriptive list of the collection and in appropriate publications.

34.3 Many archives services rely on the goodwill of depositors for support in attracting collections, in fund raising activities and in the work of Friends' groups. Such goodwill is an invaluable asset and should be fostered and acknowledged.

34.4 Depositors who present archives services with collections of outstanding value should not be expected to provide funding for the work of the archives service unless it is their express wish to do so.

35. ACCESS TO DEPOSITED COLLECTIONS BY DEPOSITORS

35.1 The archives service must facilitate personal access to a deposited collection by its depositor, or by that person's nominee, but under circumstances compatible with the procedures and standards which apply in the archives service, and compatible with the deposit agreement.

Services to users

36 PUBLICATIONS

36.1 Archives services should disseminate information in a published form for the purpose of informing researchers about the sources available and providing them with reference information. A range of publications of use to researchers includes the guide, annual report, various lists, calendars, catalogues and indexes. Publications are a means by which the wider public can become aware of archives, and derive enjoyment and benefit from the information which they contain.

36.2 The production of publications is time-consuming and necessitates considerable investment of the archivist's time during the period of their preparation.

Selection of publications on archives

36.3 Archives services should plan a publications programme which will allow for annual expenditure. Publications can also be produced in conjunction with other archives services and professional organisations.

36.4 Publications can be in a variety of physical forms. The traditional printed publication is used by many archives services although, increasingly, certain types of publication are produced in non-textual format, such as microform and CD-ROM.

36.5 The most important publication of an archives service is the guide. Guides can be designated as comprehensive, class, sectional or union. The purpose of the guide is to provide researchers with a summary of each collection or part of a collection. New editions of guides can be published at intervals by an archives service. Their content should be updated between editions by information published in annual reports about recent accessions. Those which are published in non-textual format lend themselves particularly well to being updated.

36.6 Calendars which contain transcripts or diplomatically acceptable abstracts of series of documents, and edited texts of individual documents may also be published. This type of publication is only suitable for documents of appropriate origin and age. It demands the highest standards of editorial competence. Microfilm is a suitable alternative to the traditional printed form for publishing series of archives of recent origin.

36.7 Sectional lists, which are select lists of documents from a variety of collections relating to particular subject areas, may also be published.

36.8 Catalogues of non-written archives such as maps are also published. Their publication depends on the quality and quantity of the archives in question and suitability for descriptive treatment in catalogue form.

36.9 Administrative histories which unravel the complexities of administration can also be published. The archives service has a particular responsibility to publish reference information of this kind because of the archivist's extensive knowledge of the development, structure and functioning of administration and of the records it generates.

36.10 Archives services also publish or contribute to publications which seek to develop research methodology. This is particularly important with reference to the use of information preserved in more technical or complex forms, such as electronic information.

36.11 Other publications of general interest may be produced which are often richly illustrated by the facsimile reproduction of documents, maps and photographs and contain extensive editorial comment and analysis.

36.12 Exhibition catalogues are published in the context of exhibition organisation and packs of educational facsimiles are published in the context of educational and schools services *(see 37.11.2 and section 38)*.

36.13 Publications which outline management, policy and strategic information are produced in the form of annual reports and corporate plans.

36.14 General details of archives services and of the resources and facilities which they offer to researchers may be published in directories of archives. Consideration should also be given to the use of the World Wide Web on the Internet.

36.15 Archives services also publish promotional leaflets and other leaflets which facilitate the use and understanding of archives by researchers and by the public.

37. *EXHIBITION OF ARCHIVES*

37.1 GENERAL

37.1.1 The public exhibition of archives is recommended as a means of bringing the holdings of the archives to a wider audience. An in-house exhibition area is desirable, but where this is not feasible an outside venue may be used. Archives should be exhibited in premises offering the same environmental conditions and the same levels of security against fire and theft as the strongrooms where they are normally stored. In addition, stringent lighting conditions will apply *(see 37.6)*. If these conditions cannot be provided, good quality reproductions should be exhibited instead. The archivist must have overall control of the exhibition and may call on specialist advice in technical and design areas.

37.2 THE VENUE

37.2.1 The exhibition venue should be selected in consultation with the archives service's insurers. The venue should afford a high level of protection for the documents on display and should ensure public safety.

37.3 SECURITY AGAINST THEFT

37.3.1 Original documents which are on public display are at risk of being stolen. For this reason, documents should be exhibited in locked display cabinets and the exhibition should be constantly invigilated by attendants when it is open to the public. Recording video cameras may be used to supplement personal invigilation, but should not be used as a substitute for it.

37.3.2 The exhibition venue should be fitted with an intruder alarm to Irish standard IS 199 and this should be switched on when the exhibition is closed to the public. Procedures for responding to the intruder alarm should be put in place. Recording video cameras may be used to invigilate the exhibition venue when closed to the public.

37.3.3 Display cabinets should be fitted with, at a minimum, four-level cylinder locks and should be designed so that the key-holes are concealed. The cabinets should be fitted with laminated glass set in frames designed to prevent forcible entry.

37.4 SECURITY AGAINST FIRE

37.4.1 The exhibition venue should be fitted with smoke detectors linked to a fire alarm. The venue should be furnished with fire extinguishers and attendants should be trained in their use. The venue should also be fitted with an automatic fire extinguishing system. Adequate procedures should be established for staff to respond to fire alarm calls.

37.5 ENVIRONMENTAL CONTROL

37.5.1 The venue for the exhibition should be fully air-conditioned, with temperature and relative humidity levels kept constant. BS 5454 recommends that temperature be kept within the range 13°C to 18°C and relative humidity within the range 55% to 65%.

37.5.2 If the exhibition venue is not air-conditioned, the display cabinets should be treated by a conservation professional to produce the correct levels of relative humidity for the documents.

37.5.3 Each display cabinet should contain a dial or electronic hygrometer showing the level of relative humidity within the cabinet. The hygrometer should be re-calibrated regularly. Only high quality instruments should be used for this purpose.

37.6 LIGHTING

37.6.1 All documents are liable to deteriorate when exposed to light and this is the most serious hazard arising from the public display of archives. Photography and video recordings should be strictly prohibited in the exhibition area.

37.6.2 Ultra-violet light, which is present in daylight and in the light from fluorescent lamps, offers the most serious danger to documents. Sunlight should be excluded by screening off any windows in the exhibition venue. Tungsten-filament lamps, which emit relatively small amounts of ultra-violet light, are recommended for use in exhibitions. If fluorescent lighting is used, each lamp should be fitted with an ultra-violet filter cutting off light of wave-length shorter than 400 nm. Optical fibre lighting is recommended where archives are exhibited on a long term or permanent basis.

37.6.3 Lamps should be sited outside display cabinets, to avoid a build-up of heat within the cabinets.

37.6.4 The level of light falling on each document should not exceed 50 lux. This illuminance can be measured with a light meter or by an electronic system. Lamps should be fitted with a dimmer switch to facilitate control of light levels.

37.7 CONSTRUCTION & FITTING OF DISPLAY CABINETS

37.7.1 Display cabinets should be constructed from materials which will protect the exhibits while allowing them to be viewed in comfort and safety by the public. For maximum security, cabinets should be made with a secure frame to which external wood veneers may be fitted for aesthetic reasons. Glass should be laminated, for public safety and to secure the exhibits. Cabinets should be balanced so that they are not liable to topple over.

Exhibition cases

***(below)* Wall mounted exhibition cases**

37.7.2 The interior of display cabinets should be constructed from and lined with materials which will not damage exhibits. Recommended materials include metals, glass, ceramics, inorganic pigments, polyethylene, acrylic sheets and undyed cotton, silk and linen. Materials to be avoided include tweed and wood, especially oak, birch and beech, all of which emit organic acid vapours.

37.8 DISPLAY OF DOCUMENTS

37.8.1 Documents should not be displayed in the same cabinet as metal or wooden objects, costumes or archaeological finds, especially human and animal remains. Documents may be displayed in the same cabinet as printed volumes, if the binding of such volumes does not contain metal clasps. The archivist must ensure that acceptable archival display standards are not undermined by design considerations.

37.8.2 Single documents should be displayed horizontally. They should be supported on acid-free board and be retained in place by straps made of suitable material such as cellulose acetate, polyethylene, silk, cotton or linen. These straps must be attached to the board and not to the document.

37.8.3 If a seal is attached to a document on display, it should be supported by a mount which will take the weight of the seal, thus releasing pressure on seal cords.

37.8.4 Bound manuscript volumes should never be displayed upright, as this will put a strain on the binding, especially on the spine. Bound volumes should be placed in a horizontal position and should be supported by a cradle made of acid-free board lined with chemically inert sponge. To minimise strain, bound volumes should not be opened fully-flat but at a angle not more than 25° from the horizontal. Straps used to hold the volume open should be attached to the cradle and made of suitable material.

37.9 CAPTIONS FOR EXHIBITS

37.9.1 Captions should be typed or printed on acid-free paper or board. Typefaces should be large enough to be read easily at a distance.

37.9.2 The amount of information to be contained on captions will depend on space available. At a minimum, each caption should state the title of the document; its covering dates; the material from which it is made, for example, paper or parchment; the name of the archives service where it is held; and the document reference number. Further information can be included in an exhibition catalogue *(see 37.11.2)*.

37.10 Public safety

37.10.1 The exhibition venue should be easily accessible to the public. Ideally, it should be located on the ground floor, with ramps provided for wheelchair access. If the exhibition venue is located on an upper storey of a building, then access should be provided by means of a lift.

37.10.2 1 The exhibition venue must be provided with adequate fire exits, which should be clearly marked. Staff, especially attendants, must be trained in procedures for evacuating the public in the event of fire.

37.10.3 The number of people who can be admitted to an exhibition at any one time is governed by safety factors. The minimum allocation of floor space is 1 square metre per adult, and 0.75 square metre per child, exclusive of display cabinets and any other furniture standing on the floor of the venue. Fire regulations should be consulted regarding the safety of disabled visitors *(see appendix 1)*.

37.11 Publicity

37.11.1 Publicity is essential to the success of any exhibition. This can be generated by means of posters and leaflets, which should state the title of the exhibition, its venue, opening hours and any admission charges. Leaflets are more cost-effective than posters and can achieve a wider circulation. A formal opening ceremony for the exhibition gains media attention and is a public forum for thanking sponsors and others who have provided assistance.

37.11.2 If time and resources permit, a catalogue can be produced to accompany the exhibition. The most basic catalogue consists of a typescript list of items on display. A complete printed catalogue will list all items on display, giving their historic context, a description of each item with its collection reference number, and may be fully-illustrated with colour and/or monochrome photographs. Sponsorship may be sought to meet the costs of producing the catalogue.

37.12 Lending & borrowing documents

37.12.1 When lending original documents to other organisation for exhibition purposes, the archivist should be satisfied that the exhibition venue meets the conditions of security, lighting and environmental control, which have been outlined above. The archivist should also consult the archives service's insurers. If the documents which have been requested are not the property of the archives service, it may be necessary to obtain permission from the depositors, subject to the terms and conditions of the deposit agreement.

37.12.2 Documents which are being lent for exhibition must be packed prior to transport by a conservator under the archivist's supervision. The packaging should include preconditioned silica gel to offset variations in relative humidity while in transit.

37.12.3 The archivist, or a designated member of archives staff, must accompany the documents in transit to and from the exhibition venue.

37.12.4 Documents of exceptional rarity and value are especially vulnerable to theft while in transit and may require a security guard or police presence.

37.12.5 The organisation which is borrowing original documents should be responsible for their insurance while in transit and should cover all transport and courier costs. The borrowing organisation should also arrange and pay for any security presence which may be required by the lender.

37.12.6 If documents are being sent for exhibition outside the State, an export licence must first be obtained from the relevant authority by the archives service which is lending the documents.

37.12.7 Content of captions relating to items on loan should be drawn up or approved by the archivists in advance.

37.12.8 Acknowledgments to the lending institutions or to depositors of documents being lent should be agreed in writing prior to the exhibition, and should be strictly observed by the borrowing institution. Any failure to comply with agreed acknowledgments may be constituted as a breach of contract.

37.12.9 Original documents which have been lent for exhibition should not be reproduced by the borrower without first obtaining written permission from the archives service or depositors. The archives service or the depositors whom it represents, retains copyright in such reproductions and all acknowledgments or royalties required should be honoured by the borrowing organisation in relation to exhibition catalogues or any publicity material, such as postcards or posters.

38. *EDUCATION SERVICES AND OUTREACH ACTIVITIES*

38.1 The provision of outreach activities by the archives service introduces it to a wider public and can be an important adjunct to the educational system.

38.2 The use of original documents by students is becoming increasingly common in second-level education, placing additional demands on archives services. Ideally, the archives service should be in a position to take on secondment an experienced teacher as an education officer. Where this is not possible, a member of the professional staff should be designated as education officer, with responsibility for liaison with schools, arranging for supervised group visits, and the preparation of reproduction document packs to meet the ongoing needs of changing curricula. A designated area should be provided for this service.

38.3 An introduction to original sources and the methodology of using them should be provided for third-level and post-graduate students by their faculty. It is not the function of the archives service to organise such courses or to supervise third-level students and post-graduate researchers, but individual archivists may and should make a contribution.

38.4 Continuing education courses may also require access to the facilities of the archives service in consultation with an archivist.

38.5 In addition to publications, exhibitions and education facilities, there are many other ways of promoting the archives service and reaching a wider public. Activities such as lecture series, history quizzes and group visits to the archives service, together with participation by staff members in radio and television programmes, can all extend the scope of the archives service. Developing a site on the World Wide Web also has great outreach possibilities.

APPENDIX 1

Select Bibliography

GENERAL REFERENCE WORKS:

Christopher Kitching, *Archives Buildings in the United Kingdom, 1977-1992,* The Royal Commission on Historical Manuscripts, 1993

Michel Duchein, *Les Bâtiments D'Archives, Construction et Equipements,* Archives Nationales (Paris), 1985

A Standard for Record Repositories, The Royal Commission on Historical Manuscripts, 1990

Michael Roper, *Directory of National Standards Relating to Archives Administration and Records Management,* RAMP, 1986

GUIDELINES:

Draft Guidelines for Places of Deposit for Departmental Records, National Archives, 1990

REGULATIONS RELATING TO HEALTH & FIRE SAFETY:

Code of Practice for the Management of Fire Safety in Places of Assembly, Department of the Environment, 1989

Code of Practice for Fire Safety of Furnishing and Fittings in Places of Assembly, Department of the Environment, 1989

Building Regulations, Department of the Environment, 1988

Tobacco (Health, Promotion and Protection Act), 1988, Regulations 1990 and 1995

Building Regulations (Northern Ireland): Technical Booklet `E' 1994

Fire Service Order Applicable to Designated Premises (Northern Ireland), 1984

LEGISLATION:

National Archives Act, 1986

Public Records (Northern Ireland) Act, 1923

Data Protection Act, 1988

Local Government Act, 1994

Freedom of Information Bill, 1996 (draft)

STANDARDS:

GENERAL

BS 5454
Storage and Exhibition of Archival Documents, 1989

FIRE PROTECTION

ANSI/NFPA 232AM
Guide for fire protection of archives and records centres, 1991 edition

NFPA 232
Standard for the Protection of Records, 1995 edition

NFPA 13
Installation of Sprinkler Systems, 1994 edition

ANSI/NFPA 25
Standard for the Inspection, Testing, and Maintenance of Water-Based Fire Protection Systems, 1995 edition

BS 5306
Fire extinguishing installations and equipment on premises - Part 1 Hydrant systems, hose reels and foam inlets, 1976 - *Part 2 Specification for sprinkler systems,* 1990 - *Part 3 Code of practice for selection, installation and maintenance of portable fire extinguishers,* 1985

BS 5423
Specification for portable fire extinguishers, 1987

BS 5588
Precautions in the design and construction of buildings - Part 9 Code of practice for ventilation and air conditioning duct work, 1989

BS 5839
Fire detection and alarm systems in buildings - Part 1 Code of practice for installation and servicing, 1988

BS/EN 671
Fixed Fire Fighting Systems: Part 1 Hose Systems/Reels with Semi-rigid Hose, 1995

SHELVING

BS 826
Specification for steel single tier bolted shelving (angle upright type), 1978

SECURITY

IS 199
Intruder Alarm Systems, 1987

BS 3621
Thief Resistant Locks, 1980

MICROFILM AND PHOTOGRAPHS

ANSI IT9.2-1991
Imaging media - Photographic processed films, plates, and papers - Filing enclosures and storage containers

ANSI IT9.5-1992
Imaging media (film) - Ammonia-processed diazo films - specifications for stability

ANSI/ISO 543-1990, ANSI IT9.6-1991
Photography - Photographic films - Specifications for safety films

ANSI/NAPM IT9.1-1992
Imaging media (film) - Silver-gelatin type - specifications for stability

ANSI/NAPM IT9.11-1993
American National Standard for Imaging Media - Processed Safety Photographic Films - Storage

BS/ISO 6199
Micrographics: microfilming of documents on 16 mm and 35 mm silver-gelating microfilm. Operating procedures, 1991

BS 6498
Guide to preparation of microfilm and other microforms that may be required as evidence, 1991

BS 6660
Guide to setting up and maintaining micrographics units, 1991

ISO 6051-1986 (E)
International Standard for Photography - Processed Photographic Paper Prints - Storage Practices

ISO 3897 -1986 (E)
International Standard for Photography - Processed Photographic Plates - Storage Practices

ISO 5466 -1986 (E)
International Standard for Photography - Processed Safety Photographic Film - Storage Practices

CONSERVATION

BS 4971
Repair and Allied Processes for the Conservation of Documents - Part 1 Treatment of Sheets, Membranes and Seals, 1988 - Part 2 Archival Binding, 1980

ARCHIVAL DIRECTORIES, GUIDES AND PUBLICATIONS:

Catholic Archives Society, *Directory of Catholic Archives in the United Kingdom and Eire,* 1984

Clark, M. and Refaussé, R., *Directory of Historic Dublin Guilds,* Dublin, 1993

Connolly, P. and Martin, G., *The Dublin Guild Merchant Roll,* Dublin, 1992

Corr, S., Rourke, G.D. and McParland, M., *Irish Conservation Directory*, 1988

Helferty, S. and Refaussé, R., *Directory of Irish Archives*, Dublin, 1993

Lohan, R., *Guide to the Archives of the Office of Public Works,* Dublin, 1994

Refaussé, R. ed., *The Register of the Parish of St. Thomas,* Dublin 1750 to 1791, Dublin, 1995

Ward-Perkins, S., *Select Guide to Trade Union Records in Dublin,* Dublin, 1996

APPENDIX 2

Society of Archivists Code of Conduct

In 1994, the members of the Society of Archivists agreed, by ballot, to the introduction of a binding code of conduct, as a condition of membership of the Society, to take effect from 1 October 1994.

PURPOSE

The purpose of The Code of Conduct is to set out the standards of professional behaviour expected of archivists, archive conservators, records managers and those occupied in related activities who are members of the Society of Archivists. No exhaustive code of conduct can be laid down to cover all situations. However, the Council of the Society is always available to give guidance to members: members have a duty to obtain a ruling, through the Honorary Secretary of the Society, on all occasions when they are in doubt as to the proper standards of professional behaviour.

GENERAL GUIDELINES

The Code of Conduct sets out certain basic principles that are intended to help members maintain the highest standards of professional conduct. Should a case arise where a member is believed to have fallen short of the standards desired, procedures are defined within the Articles of the Association of the Society *(Articles 20 to 27)* and within the Bye-Laws of the Society *(Section 10)* which permit the convening of a Disciplinary Panel.

STANDARD REQUIREMENT

All applicants for membership of the Society are required to sign an undertaking that they will abide by The Code of Conduct if elected.

The Code of Conduct of the Society of Archivist is as follows:

a) Members must seek to promote the objects of the Society as set out in its Memorandum and Articles of Association, and must not engage in any action which is contrary to those objects.

b) Members of the Society must conduct themselves in such a way that their behaviour would not reasonably be regarded by the Council of the Society as professional misconduct.

c) Members must endeavour to develop their professional understanding and expertise, to contribute to extending the body of professional knowledge and to ensure that those whose training or activities they supervise are equipped to carry out their tasks in a competent manner.

d) Members must act with due regard to the Society's Equal Opportunities Policy and not discriminate in their dealings with individuals, or organisations on the grounds of race, colour, religious beliefs or practices, ethnic or national origin, disabilities, gender, marital status and age.

e) Members must refrain from activities that might prejudice their professional integrity and, in particular, must ensure that private research and publication, personal collecting interests or collaboration with the media do not conflict with or encroach upon their professional responsibilities.

f) Members must perform their function in respect of the creation, maintenance and disposal of current and semi-current records, the selection, acceptance or acquisition of records for archival custody, the safeguarding, preservation and conservation of records in their care and the arrangement, description, publication and making available for use of those records in accordance with generally accepted archival principles and practices, offering impartial advice to all and employing available resources to provide a balanced range of services.

g) Members must not misuse or allow unauthorised disclosure or use of any information acquired by them in confidence in the course of their professional work.

h) The primary duty of members is to maintain the integrity of the records in their care and custody, but in performing this duty they must balance the respective legitimate rights and interests of employers, owners, data subjects and users, both present and future.

i) Members must seek to avoid conflict with their professional colleagues and with members of related professions and strive to resolve difficulties by agreement on a basis of mutual respect and understanding.

j) Members must not seek or seem to ascribe to the Society responsibility for views expressed or actions taken by them unless expressly authorised to do so.

All enquiries concerning The Code of Conduct should be addressed to the Honorary Secretary of the Society of Archivists.

Index